Now, Whose Fault Is That?

Now, Whose Fault Is That?

The Struggle for Self-Esteem In the Face of Chronic Unemployment

Cato Wadel

Newfoundland Social and Economic Studies No. 11

Institute of Social and Economic Research,
Memorial University of Newfoundland

©Institute of Social and Economic Research
Memorial University of Newfoundland 1973
St. John's, Newfoundland, Canada
ISBN 0-919666-05-1
Seventh Printing 1982

Contents

Foreword

This study, whose originality and integrity will surely win recognition from a wide audience, culminates Mr. Cato Wadel's research on the Newfoundland scene, at least for the time being. The report from his previous major field research project in Newfoundland is already published as volume 7 in these *Studies*; Mr. Wadel is also a contributor and co-editor of volume 5 of the *Papers*, and is involved in the preparation of a volume planned on the politics of Newfoundland. On behalf of the Institute and his many colleagues here, I wish to thank Cato Wadel for this present volume and his other stimulating contributions to the research programme and professional *milieu* of the Institute. He is now Associate Professor of Social Anthropology at the University of Tromsö in his native Norway.

This book has been published with the help of a grant from the Social Science Research Council of Canada, using funds provided by the Canada Council.

Toronto
May, 1973

Robert Paine
Director of Sociological Research
Institute of Social and Economic Research
Memorial University of Newfoundland

Preface

This study was made possible through the financial help of the Institute of Social and Economic Research at Memorial University of Newfoundland. For this help I wish to express my gratitude to the Governing Committee of the Institute.

In writing up the material I received helpful criticism from several colleagues and friends. I am especially indebted to David Alexander, Jean Briggs, Kenneth Burridge, Anthony Cohen, Harald Eidheim, Clinton Herrick, Robert Paine, and George Park. I am also indebted to Sonia Kuryliw Paine and George Story for their editorial work.

I also want to thank my wife, Synnöve, for her encouragement and assistance during the field work and writing periods. Not being an academic herself, she insisted that I write a book which non-academics could appreciate and a book which would convey what my informants had to say. I hope that I have succeeded in doing this, to some extent.

Finally, I want to thank the people of Squid Cove and particularly George and Elizabeth for their hospitality, help, and co-operation. I am well aware that I have written about persons with whom I had friendships but whom I not always told exactly what I was up to. I cannot know if they will be pleased with what I have written. My hope – and excuse – is that it may contribute to an understanding of their problems and that this understanding in turn may have some influence in improving the situation of those citizens who in spite of our welfare states, tend to fall outside them due to prolonged unemployment.

Tromsö,
January, 1973

Cato Wadel

Introduction

I'm willin' to work but there's no work around.
Now, whose fault is that?

This book is about the ways in which men adapt to unemployment in a rural area of a 'welfare state.' More specifically, it focuses upon able-bodied men experiencing long-term or chronic unemployment, and as a result, have to live off public welfare or "on the dole."

The deprivation, through the inability to secure employment, is not only – indeed, not primarily – a matter of income deficiency. Although income from various welfare sources does not generally compete, even in the most progressive welfare states, with income from work (since welfare laws have generally "been designed on the basis of an essentially negative philosophy: that of discouraging idleness" [Gladwin, 1967:69]), in some marginal rural areas of many a welfare state, income from various welfare sources combined with a varied subsistence production may closely approach income from unskilled work. The latter statement in fact, describes the area with which this study is concerned; namely, rural Newfoundland which benefits from welfare regulations largely calculated on the basis of an urban and 'mainland' Canadian situation. Rural Newfoundland may thus, in a way, represent an important case in evaluating the economic versus the social component of deprivation related to unemployment.

The basis for the social deprivation or stigma resulting from long-term unemployment seems to be the insistence that a man should earn his living and that a man is, himself, primarily responsible for his own economic condition. There seem to be few exceptions to this rule; those who are exempted and socially accepted are the sick, the old, the young, and one may add, the idle rich, who have independent means. That no work is available is generally not an *immediately* acceptable excuse for the unemployed themselves, or for those with whom the unemployed might interact, or for the society at large. I shall discuss the reasons for this throughout the book. At this stage, I would like to stress another point; namely, that there is likely to be some discrepancy between the views of the unemployed themselves and those of others in this respect: the unemployed will accept excuses more readily (that "work is scarce,") than those who are employed. In other words, the unemployed man is likely to be involved in an argument with others within his community and society at large about the causes for his unemployment. However, to succeed in such an argument, the unemployed person is required to ascribe to certain rules; for example, to restrict his interaction with other unemployed men, and engage in subtle forms of 'impression management' (Goffman, 1959), especially regarding his willingness to work.

Moreover, the unemployed man's arguments are concerned not only with the causes of his unemployment, but also with reducing the all-importance of the work-role in the evaluation of his social and personal worth. Thus, he is often found over-communicating other roles where his score may be high, including those in his *past* working career, his poor health or 'sick role' (especially when caused by strain in former jobs), his family (husband and father) roles, his friend and neighbour roles, and, indeed, his local class role; that is, his position in relation to other less excusable unemployed people.

Furthermore, the arguments which the unemployed are involved in take place in a changing field of interpersonal relations. Becoming unemployed inevitably means immediate changes in one's interpersonal network. These changes are likely to occur in terms of affective *content* with people one continues to see (for example, the family), as well as in terms of *personnel*; for example, the loss of relations with workmates and the expanding relations with various officials, such as the welfare officer and the doctor.

Changes in the content of the interpersonal relations of the unemployed, especially those within the family, have been the concern of several writers (cf. Cavan and Ranck, 1938; Bakke, 1940; Cavan, 1959). In this study, I am not primarily occupied with the change of content and with the reversal of the husband and wife roles, partly because the wife does not become the 'breadwinner' in Squid Cove. (This seems to be one basic difference between rural and urban situations of unemployment.) Rather, my emphasis will be on the changes in the network of interpersonal relations outside the nuclear family in what may be termed the secondary field of interpersonal relations. Such relations include secondary kin, friends, neighbours, and workmates; their relevance to the unemployed is that they seem to provide the most important field for social acceptance and evaluation of self.[1]

The primary data on which the study is based have been gathered through participant observation fieldwork for twelve months during 1967, 1968, and 1969 in a number of small rural, or what are locally called, "outport" communities in northeastern Newfoundland. Newfoundland became the tenth province of Canada in 1949 and as such, came to share in the many social benefits of the Canadian welfare state. The new province also became subject to a modernization process emphasizing industrialization, urbanization, and a resettlement of the rural communities. I have tried to show else-

1   Like Goffman (1963), I shall be especially concerned with "mixed contacts"; that is, interactions between unemployed (stigmatized) and employed (normals). Unlike Goffman, I shall be as much concerned with interaction between people who have known each other for a life-time as with interaction between strangers. This is again related to the rural base of my material.

where how this modernization process, while bringing increased material prosperity to the majority of the province's population, at the same time has been instrumental in increasing unemployment and putting a large minority on public relief. (See Wadel, 1969a; also Skolnik and Wadel, 1969.) In this study, I shall not be concerned with how individuals *become* unemployed nor with policy strategies to restrict unemployment; rather, I shall focus on how individuals and families manage the situation of unemployment, after becoming unemployed.

Although this study is based on personal contact with about a hundred unemployed welfare recipients (as well as with several non-recipients)[2] from a dozen small outports, the study centres around the situation of one man whom I call George, and his family. The reasons for choosing such an approach are several: first, George and his family were my next-door neighbours for six months of the fieldwork and during this time, we interacted daily; George came to regard me as a 'friend' to whom he could talk openly about his situation and whom he could include in his network of personal relations. Not unexpectedly, I found that most welfare recipients were very hesitant to "open up" their network so that I managed to participate on a personal basis with only a dozen families. Thus, a basic reason for choosing the case approach was due to the difficulty of securing intimate data on the 'delicate' subject of being on welfare.

A second reason for choosing the case approach is based on my dissatisfaction with the correlative method adopted in many sociological and economic studies of the unemployed. Such studies have invariably identified a number of factors correlating with unemployment; for example, low level of education, low degree of skill, large and disorganized families, poor health, poor housing, and particularly in Newfoundland, residence in small rural (outport) communities. These characteristics have, in turn, been found to correlate with a number of negative personality characteristics such as apathy, dependency, and a rejection of the work ethic. On this basis, it has been common – even if not intended by the researchers – for the public at large, including the media, to impute a simple cause-and-effect relation with

2   The data collected included "career" histories, the present employment situation, the family situation, educational and skill levels, networks of interpersonal relations for the unemployed as well as for their employed neighbours and friends. Complete censuses were taken partly with the help of local field assistants for five communities. Besides the usual census data (household composition, age, sex, educational level, religious affiliation, occupation, ownership of house, land, and other assets) the kinship relations to other households in the community and neighbouring communities were plotted for each household. It was not possible to gather complete income data, but close approximations were made on the basis of length of work, catch statistics (for the fishermen) and family composition (for the various transfer payments, family allowance, old-age pension, unemployment insurance, and able-bodied relief). For further details on the field work see Appendix.

unemployment as the effect.[3] Besides the fact that it might very well be the
other way around, that is, that unemployment can be the cause and the
correlates the effect, little or no analysis of social interaction processes is
involved in such an approach.

A third reason arises from the view that the social processes relating
unemployment to its various concomitants are best isolated by focusing on
a subjective point of view – subjective in respect to the way in which the
unemployed themselves experience their situation and how they try to deal
with it. What seems to be crucial, if we are to appreciate the ramifications
of unemployment, are the factors responsible for what may be termed the
downward social mobility among the unemployed; that is, how the inability
to secure employment, to earn one's living, tends to lead to problems in
fulfilling other roles and in maintaining relations within one's family and
community, and in maintaining one's identity and self-respect.

A final word about the mode of presentation: the introductory chapter
aims at providing an outline of the historical setting out of which modern
rural unemployment in Newfoundland has emerged. The chapter is divided
into two sections: the first is concerned with the development of the Newfoundland economy in general, with particular emphasis on the changing
employment structure in the rural areas; the second outlines the same changes
for the community which is the focus of this study. The treatment is somewhat concise by necessity. I refer the reader who finds the treatment too
inadequate to the Newfoundland Social and Economic Studies No. 1 to 9
and the other works listed in the bibliography.

Chapter 2 through chapter 8 have, as their core, an analysis of George's
problems in maintaining his family status, his community status, and his
"class" status (cf. Barber, 1961) derived from his being unemployed and
his having to live largely off public welfare. Throughout these chapters, I
make an effort to go beyond George's problems to those of other unemployed
welfare recipients in similar as well as somewhat different circumstances.
In chapters 8 and 9, problems other than George's are examined: in chapter
8, of men residing in what may be termed welfare neighbourhoods or
ghettoes, and in chapter 9 of the children of welfare recipients and the
younger generation in general. Chapter 10 is an attempt to show the other

3 Significantly, in its Fifth Annual Review (1968:113) the Economic Council of
Canada finds it necessary to point out that "one should be careful to avoid confusing
characteristics with causes, and to bear in mind constantly how the total amount of
poverty (including unemployment and public relief) can be affected by broad,
economy-wide forces such as the rate of economic growth in relation to potential.
If the economy falls well below its potential, the incomes of many people will drop
because they become unemployed. It is highly likely under these circumstances that
unemployment will tend to strike hardest at those with least education; but to say
simply that these person's low income is *caused* by the lack of education is not an
adequate analysis of the situation."

side of the coin: how the employed people of Squid Cove regard the dilemma of their unemployed neighbours.

The chapter titles (except 9 and 10) are George's own words and correspond to the major themes of what may be referred to as his reservoir of self-esteem: his long working career (I've had twenty-nine years in the woods); his difficulties in getting employment (I'm willin' to work, but there's no work around); the fact that he is partly disabled (I'm not as strong as I used to be); that his wife and family are respected in the community (I've had a good woman); that he is working a lot for himself (I've enough to do around the house to keep me busy); that he has an extensive network of kin and friends (I've lots of friends around here); that many other men in the community do not have as many 'reserves' as he has (I'm better off than many around here); and finally, that his children have done relatively well (I wants every education I can get).

The Setting

The settlement and historic growth of Newfoundland occurred mainly as a consequence of the tremendous lucrative cod fishery in nearby waters. From the earliest settlement in the seventeenth century until well into the twentieth century, the economy centred around the inshore fishery. The adaptation to inshore fishing resulted in a dispersed population among coastal islands and headlands in a plethora of small fishing villages generally referred to as outports.

The distinguishing feature of the Newfoundland inshore fishery was and is its seasonality. Except for the South Coast of Newfoundland, local and arctic ice make fishing almost impossible for four to five months of the year. Moreover, the high season, that is the cod run in mid-summer, lasts only a couple of months when the cod come "right into the rocks."

The technology required to exploit these resources was and still is relatively simple; wooden skiffs rarely exceeding 30 feet in length and fishing gear such as hand lines, nets, and the so-called cod-trap.[1] The trap can yield very high catches; half a million pounds for an eight-week season is not uncommon. During the season, the trap can thus be efficient in terms of return, both per unit of labour and capital.

The fishing crew comprises from one to six men (trap crews) and are typically made up of at least a core of close kin (a father and his son(s) or a group of brothers). A single household thus often has more than one income earner. The choice of technology is largely determined by the availability of close kin.

In spite of the potentially high productivity of the fishery, the uncertainty of the catch and the shortness of the season mean that it cannot be counted on to provide enough income for the whole year. Traditionally this situation was largely compensated by an extensive subsistence production including a variety of vegetable, animal, forest, and marine products. Subsistence pro-

---

1 The cod trap is a net or linet box having four sides, a bottom but no top. It is set off shore, the distance depending on the depth of the water and the nature of the bottom in shoal water. On the shore side of the trap there is an opening or door. From the centre of this opening is a net (the leader) extending to the shore. The entire trap is moored to shore and buoyed up by wooden kegs or cork floats. The principle of the trap is simple: cod moves inshore to feed upon the spawing caplin. As a school of cod moves along the shoreline they encounter the leader, which causes them to turn with the direction of the leader, into the trap (see Philbrook, 1966:60–61).

duction appears to have contributed as much to the real income of the outport household as the fishery.[2]

The extensiveness of the above activities and the process of curing fish in the sun were made possible only through the co-operation of all members of the household; the housewife as well as the children joined in the labour. This co-operation was necessary not only because of the magnitude and diversity of the work, but also because both the fishery and the agricultural activities took place during the same summer months.

The so-called Labrador fishery can also be classified as an inshore fishery. The Newfoundland fishermen taking part in this fishery in the summer months were either "floaters" (those who fished from schooners) or "stationers" (those who fished from the shore). The stationers travelled to the Labrador coast with all their equipment on board coastal steamers. The schooners were generally built locally and weighed between 30 and 70 tons. The schooners were not usually used for the actual fishing but rather for the transport of men (between five and fifteen), fishing equipment (dories and traps), and of course the fish. The Labrador schooners were owned and operated by fish merchants as well as by local skippers. Some merchants could own a great number of schooners themselves and "outfit" an even larger number owned by local skippers. (See Black, 1960:267–93 for a detailed description of the Labrador fishery.)

Traditionally, all trade with the larger society was controlled by the outport fish merchant, and conducted almost entirely on a credit basis. Each spring the fisherman approached the merchant in order to obtain an "outfit" on credit, thereby making the merchant share the risk of the fishery. Throughout the summer, fishing equipment and consumer goods would be added to this account. At the end of the fishing season, the cured fish were taken to the merchant to be sorted, weighed, and appraised according to quality and price, and all entries on the accounts were deducted from the value of the fish. On the balance, if there was one, the fisherman would take out his winter supplies of a limited number of consumer goods.

In theory, a fisherman could take his catch to any merchant, be paid in cash and then pay his original outfitter. However, in practice, most communities had only one merchant and when there were several, they often made non-competitive arrangements with each other. The credit relationship between a fisherman and 'his' merchant would generally continue for years, not uncommonly over the generations, and typically wholly on a

---

2 Subsistence production included vegetables such as potatoes, turnips, cabbage, carrots, beets, parsnips, peas, and beans; animal products from cows, sheep, pigs, goats and chickens; marine products such as cod, herring, salmon, caplin, lobster, seals, and sea birds; firewood and building material from forest products; and hunting game (moose, rabbits, and various birds).

non-cash basis. Some of the older Newfoundlanders are said not to have seen money before World War II.

Indeed, the non-cash basis of the exchange itself perpetuated the credit relationship. The accounting seems to have been secondary, symbolizing the necessity of the relationship rather than determining it (Szwed, 1966:43). If the catch was bad, the fisherman would be in debt and the merchant would normally 'carry' him; that is, supply him with the basic necessities over the winter, relying on the fishery of subsequent years to make up the balance. The system thus gave some security to the fisherman, the merchant acting as a buffer between him and the fluctuating world markets for fish.

The fishermen themselves had neither the skill nor the organization and capital to involve themselves in marketing and financing. Data from other countries where fishermen have succeeded in re-organizing and gaining some control over marketing, for example in Iceland and Norway, suggest that this would have to be done on a nation-wide basis and with the active support of the government.[3] In Newfoundland, the merchant 'class' had control of the government.

The outport merchants were thus more than commercial figures. Their connections with, and knowledge of, the outside world meant that they acted as advisors for the fishermen on a wide range of affairs: legal documents, travel, government regulations, education, and other problems. The merchants were also the most likely people to be patronized by administrators and politicians. This, together with their commercial activities, put them into a position of considerable potential power in the outport communities.

Every merchant-fisherman relationship was a personal dyadic contract. In the words of one informant: "There was a kind of understanding between the merchant and yourself; you could go to the merchant with a feeling that nobody would know anythin' about what you were talkin' about; it would always be only you and him in the office; you didn't deal with Brown & Sons (a fictitious name) but with Mr. John or Mr. Henry."

The fishermen did not have a *collective* relationship with the merchant. They never bargained with him as a group but only as individuals. This personalization of their interaction resulted in a classical patron-client relationship (see Wolf, 1955; 1966). The merchants took upon themselves a number of the functions which, at present, are regarded as the responsibility of governments; most important for the present theme, they gave a basic security to all the outport inhabitants and they did this through a recognized

---

3 The process of organizing the fishermen began earlier in Newfoundland than in either Iceland or Norway, viz. in 1908 under the leadership of William Coaker. The effort failed for various reasons but largely it seemed due to the resistance of the merchants. For a detailed analysis of the Coaker movement see Feltham, 1959; also Wadel, 1969a.

government technique, that of redistribution. However, unlike the present welfare system, the fishermen had to work in order to get the benefits. "The entire productive effort of the parish (outport) was absorbed by the merchants, then levelled and distributed back to the parish (outport). Production and productive 'income' was pulled to an 'average' level, while bursts of high productivity and quality, as well as non-productivity, were thwarted and even scorned" (Szwed, 1966:52). The merchants' strategies thus implied that the 'good' fishermen were paying for the possible shortcomings of their fellow fishermen.

In addition, the mercantile system had a conservative influence on the outport economic system in not promoting innovations in fishing techniques. Reorganizing the technology by the merchants would have absorbed their capital which could be spent more profitably in speculating on the fish markets. The speculative nature of the markets and the shortage of capital thus encouraged the application of short-term strategies to the exclusion of technological and organizational innovations. The merchants might indeed be said to have had an interest in the continued backwardness of the fishermen.

Moreover, this mercantile system set few restrictions on how many client-fishermen it could include. It was relatively easy for a fisherman to become self-employed with the modest capital required and the possibilities for credit. Also, when old fishing grounds became crowded, fishermen established new settlements further along the coast. The ecology, together with the mercantile system were thus capable of absorbing much of the increasing number of people who had limited possibilities of earning a living in another way.

Industrial development within Newfoundland did not begin before the end of the 19th century when a trans-island railway was completed. The railway was thought to open up the large forest resources in inland New-foundland and the lumber industry was "intended to replace the fishery as the major foundation of the Newfoundland economy" (Philbrook, 1966:6). Except for the establishment of a number of saw-mills, the forest did not become the new resource until a paper mill was built in central Newfound-land in 1909 and a second mill on the west coast in 1925. The saw-mills and the paper mills effected demographic changes; that is, migration from the fishing communities on the island and headlands into the bays and further inland, and the establishment of what eventually became specialized logger communities. In these bay and inland communities, there were limited opportunities for fishing (with the exception of lobster), but the land and forest resources for subsistence production were generally more abundant than elsewhere on the island.

Until the 1950s, the production of pulp wood was a three-phase activity governed by seasonal climatic conditions and a relatively simple technology.

(See Curran, 1971, and Peters, 1967 for a detailed analysis of the logging industry.) The first phase was the actual cutting and piling of the wood from early September to mid-December. The technological kit consisted of the buck-saw and axe, and the activities were usually performed by the same person, sometimes with a teenaged son as a work-partner.

The second phase, "the haul-off," involved the hauling of the pulp wood along frozen ground to rivers and other collecting places; this took place from early January to early or mid-March. The basis of the technology was horse and sled. The horses were owned either by the men themselves (teamsters) or by the companies. The former used their horses for other purposes at other times of the year; for example, for hauling firewood.

The third phase, the "drive," involved the transportation of the pulp wood by water directly to the mill sites or to a railway terminal for further transportation by rail. These activities took place between May and August and were performed by various work teams.

The various phases required varying amounts of labour with the cutting phase in the fall demanding the most. Largely as a result of this, woodswork came to involve two categories of labourers. The first were men from communities where local fish resources were absent. They usually participated in more than one of the phases and came to depend on logging as their main or only source of cash income. These men, whom we may call professional loggers, came from predominantly logger communities. Wage work in other sectors of the economy, notably construction, was sometimes substituted for one of the logging phases.

The seasonal breaks in the woods operations also allowed these men to take advantage of various forms of subsistence production. The break in December-January was used for "getting in" firewood; the period after "haul-off" was used to cut firewood and for preparing and planting vegetable gardens; the period after the drive was for harvesting. This neat cycle could, however, easily be disrupted by climatic changes that forced both the paper companies and the men to re-schedule the various activities.

The second category of loggers came from communities with other cash resources, notably fishing. These fishermen-loggers took part only in the cutting phase in the fall while concentrating on fishing in the summer. Moreover, some fishermen chose not to engage in logging at all and others only in some years. In many fishing communities, logging seems to have been regarded as work only for those who could not 'make it' in the fishery. Fishermen were also less likely to go logging when they had had a successful fishing season, whereas a bad season made logging necessary. Newly married and unmarried sons might also have gone logging while their fathers took care of the male household duties and the preparations for the next fishing season. If they were successful in establishing an economically viable household, they might have dropped logging. The result was that the 'wage-fund' for logging was to a great extent distributed among the fishermens' households according to need.

The combination of several occupations, an adaptation which might be called "occupational pluralism" (see Skolnik and Wadel, 1969), constituted the livelihood for most of the rural population in Newfoundland up to World War II. Except for a general decline in economic activity during the Depression, this adaptation seems to have maintained a general distribution of employment and income for most of the outport population, although there was certainly a lot of what we now call underemployment, and the income level was generally low.

During the Depression, many fishermen became hopelessly in debt to the merchants who were then unable to give credit to all. The paper companies were also hit and forced to reduce their activity. During the winter of 1932, for instance, no less than 70,000 persons, or 25 per cent of the Newfoundland population, were in receipt of some public relief (*Newfoundland Royal Commission*, 1933:83). The only expansion in the economy occurred in the subsistence sector.[4]

In 1933, because of political as well as economic factors, the self-government which Newfoundland had enjoyed within the British Commonwealth since 1855 was replaced by the rule of a Commission, appointed by and responsible to the British Government (see Perlin, 1959).

The economic situation was somewhat relieved by the late '30s, but real recovery did not come before the outbreak of World War II. With the war, the market for both fishery and forest products got a boost. Moreover, due to its strategic position, Newfoundland was chosen for the construction of several American military bases. At the peak of the construction period, no less than 19,000 Newfoundlanders, or close to 25 per cent of the total labour force, were employed at these bases. According to one Newfoundland historian, "the island began to prosper as never before" (Perlin, 1959:51).

However, little occurred during the war that could give the island a firm basis for self-sustained economic growth besides the already established resource industries. With regard to the fishing outports, one can say the contrary took place in that the traditional merchants were not able to adapt to the post-war situation and many outports lost their only (albeit paternalistic) entrepreneurs (see Wadel, 1969a:Ch. V). On the other hand, the quick and easy money that came from the war, coupled with the presence of large numbers of Canadian and American soldiers and goods, led to rapidly rising aspirations among the population. These two factors, among others, were

---

4 The opportunities for subsistence production greatly cushioned the effect of the depression in rural Newfoundland. Local production of one of the main staples, potatoes, has been estimated to have been 95 million pounds in 1921, 123 million pounds in 1935, and 90 million pounds in 1945. See Singh (1964).

behind the referenda that made Newfoundland the tenth province of Canada in 1949.

The people in the outports in general came to look upon Confederation as "the greatest thing that happened to Newfoundland." The economic benefits were felt immediately by most outport households. First, families and individuals became eligible for the full range of Canadian transfer payments – family allowances, old age pensions, and unemployment insurance – where practically none had existed before. It should be noted that the relative value of these payments was much greater in the outports than in the urban industrial setting in which there were no possibilities for subsistence production and in which living costs (for example, housing) and consumption patterns were generally higher.[5]

Secondly, the extension of various public services to Newfoundland (transportation, education, health, and public buildings) entailed, besides better services, new opportunities for employment. Many of the jobs that were created in construction did not require special skills and were thus immediately open to many outporters. Moreover, since much of the employment was local (road and school construction), it could be combined with other sources of income, notably with fishing and woodswork (occupational pluralism).

Another result was the rise of a group of 'professional' construction workers in most outports. Because most of the construction work was temporary in any one area and also seasonal, many of these workers did not change residence but continued to live in the outports.

Thirdly, with Confederation, a strong effort was initiated to bring new industries to the province offering specialized year-round jobs. However, although great progress was made by direct government action in developing some basic resource industries, few new industries emerged to produce the capital inputs for, or to utilize the output of, these industries; that is, few backward and forward domestic linkages emerged. Indeed, it seems to be a general principle that domestic linkages are not likely to emerge when the main industries are primary export industries and the population is small, in addition. Moreover, there would be considerable difficulty in establishing consumer-goods industries for import substitution in Newfoundland because of the small size of the local market and consequent inability to realize the

5 Perlin notes that "Newfoundland had nothing at the time (of Confederation) that could be conceivably compared with the social services of Canada. There were no family allowances. Old age pensions were paid to persons of 70 years and over on the basis of a means test and at the rate of $75 per year. There was no unemployment insurance. To a people whose social services were fifty years behind the times and whose subsistence economy could allow life to be endured on cash incomes often less than the family allowance would produce, the attractions (of Confederation) were seductive" (1959:54).

potential economies of scale and the preference of the local population for imported goods. Many small countries in the world face the same problem but are able to overcome it to some extent, for example, by introducing tariffs, an alternative no longer open to Newfoundland since Confederation (cf. Hirschman, 1958; Demas, 1965; Skolnik, 1966; Edgecombe, 1967). Indeed, in Newfoundland, a number of domestic industries were forced to close down as a result of Confederation. Thus, secondary manufacturing industries (excluding pulp and paper, saw-milling and fish processing) still provide employment for no more than 10 per cent of the Newfoundland labour force.

The only significant expansion in processing occurred in frozen fish fillet production. Most work in these fish plants required skills that could be acquired in a short training period in the plants and were thus open to most outporters, including women. However, the wage rates were correspondingly low and still are, averaging $1.25 an hour. Year-round employment (that is, fifty weeks at forty-five hours a week) would thus not pay more than $2,800. Moreover, plants were established only in a few larger centres, giving relatively few outport communities access to either work in the plants or possibilities for the fishermen to sell their fish. For the fish plants to have been of real significance to most outports, they would have had to be smaller and in greater numbers (see Wadel, 1969:Ch. VI).

Fourthly, and in conjunction with the establishment of fish plants, the government adopted a policy of attempting to transform the small-scale, seasonal, inshore fishery to a large-scale, deep-sea, year-round industrial fishery. Beginning with the setting up of the Newfoundland Fisheries Development Authority in 1953, the provincial government (with substantial federal aid) and the federal government independently initiated a series of fisheries programmes. While programmes prior to Confederation were primarily concerned with the marketing side of the industry, post-confederation programmes concentrated on productivity and production methods. In general terms, this meant specialization: a change to larger boats, a movement from inshore to offshore fishing, and a transition from salt fish to fresh fish. There are two separate components in this specialization process: an offshore, and a "middle ground" or near-shore development.

The near-shore development aims to provide fishermen with incentives, mainly in the form of bounties, for the acquisition of "longliners," small multi-purpose boats for fishing close to the coast. This method combines important aspects of the traditional inshore fishing with offshore techniques; it also combines well with fresh fish plants, as well as with fishermen salting the fish themselves. The offshore development has involved subsidizing the acquisition of draggers, the building of fresh fish plants, and encouraging labour to move from inshore to offshore activities.

Besides its economic importance, the emphasis on offshore development also has a (Canadian) nationalistic aspect. The size of the foreign fishing fleets operating outside Newfoundland has increased substantially during the past decade and it was felt that Canada (Newfoundland) should increase the size of its fleet proportionately in order to retain its share of its territorial waters.

In addition to the various programmes designed to modernize the fishing industry, the government has simultaneously given various kinds of assistance to the traditional inshore fishery such as bait services, a 50 per cent salt rebate, the building of community stages and harbour facilities, and various insurance and loan services. A fishermens' union, the Newfoundland Federation of Fishermen, was also established shortly after Confederation under the sponsorship of the premier. Although most of these schemes were designed to tide the inshore fishery over the modernization period, it seems apparent that they have acted as a brake on the transition and at the same time, have had limited effects on making the inshore fishery proper a more viable livelihood. Any development of the inshore fishery would have had to put priority on market organization and the raising of fish prices (see Brox, 1972).

One of the major problems facing the first provincial government was the difficulty and high cost of providing its dispersed population with modern services. Moreover, for most of these scattered communities, the main resource was inshore fishing, and there seemed to be strong indications that the inshore fishery was rapidly becoming unprofitable. These two factors seem to be the basic reasons why in 1953, the Newfoundland government inaugurated a programme to assist people in moving to larger centres. The amount of financial aid given was modest at first, the maximum being $600 per family; to obtain the money, the whole community had to certify its willingness to move. The main aim of the government seemed to be the provision of social services but, in fact, no restrictions were placed on where the people might resettle.

Under this first plan, 115 communities totalling 8,000 people resettled (Rowe 1967:76). It should be added that prior to this form of government assistance, indeed continuously throughout the past fifty years, a large number of small communities had resettled on their own account: the government thus did not initiate the centralization process.

However, the new type of resettlement did not generally lead to a change in occupation and it had little to do with economic development, a fact that is well illustrated by the material collected by Iverson and Matthews (1967). Indeed, it might be said that people often moved from one marginal community to another which, although more 'central,' often had a poorer resource base. What people lost in productive income was, however, often compensated by various transfer payments.

This fact, seems to be the basis for the introduction of a new joint federal-provincial resettlement programme in 1965. Besides an increase in the amount of money offered those willing to move, 70 per cent being supplied by federal sources, the important aspect of the new scheme was that to get the grant, one had to move to *approved* growth centres. The shift in emphasis from "providing services" to "fruitful employment" was also indicated by the fact that the administration of the programme was transferred from the Department of Welfare to the Department of Fisheries. Under this joint plan which lasted until June 1967, about 68 communities comprising nearly 5,000 people were resettled, many to communities where fish plants were in operation (Rowe, *op. cit.*).

The early post-confederation years were characterized by great optimism regarding employment: it was felt that the inshore fishery, other seasonal work, and subsistence production could be replaced completely by full-time specialized jobs. The premier who led Newfoundland into Confederation (he remained premier until 1972), J. R. Smallwood, is widely reputed to have advised the fishermen: "Pull up your boats, burn your flakes, and forget the (inshore) fishery; there will be two jobs for every man in Newfoundland."[6]

Until 1957, the optimism was not thoroughly stifled. While unemployment during the first two years of Confederation had been high (13.3 per cent), in the following six years (1951–56) it averaged only 6 per cent. The first post-war decade also saw a substantial drop in the number of inshore fishermen, from 31,600 in 1945 to 14,300 in 1956 (Rowe: *op. cit.*). Most of the former fishermen found new employment in the expanding construction and transportation industries involved in upgrading the public services and in fish-processing.

However, many people were not able to secure employment for the whole year either in the new occupations or by combining traditional and new occupations. No less than a third of the labour force (35,000 of 101,000 in 1957), urban as well as rural, was dependent upon unemployment insurance benefits as its major or only source of income during the winter months. Seasonality and consequently, reliance on unemployment insurance characterized all available niches: traditional occupations as well as construction, transportation, and other service industries (see Hurwitz, 1966).

The economy of the new province was still vulnerable and highly dependent on financial help from federal sources. As Perlin wrote in the mid-1950s, "it has been generally agreed that financial assistance on a very substantial scale will be required to allow the province to continue its public services at their present levels and standards" (*op. cit.*, p. 62). If one were to include employment in the "public services," one would find that a sub-

6   In 1972, Smallwood gave this as an example of a statement attributed to him which he never, in fact, made.

stantial proportion of the Newfoundland labour force, perhaps 25 per cent, owed their employment directly to federal spending.

However, in the second half of the 1950s, the employment situation worsened drastically. "Beginning with the recession (in the North American economy) in early 1957, Newfoundland experienced a severe slow-down in activity which prevailed into the early '60s. Employment figures averaged 101,000 at this time, only 5,000 greater than the average from 1951 to 1956. At the same time, the labour force increased by 17,000. As a result, the unemployment rate soared to an average of almost 16 per cent, reaching a peak of nearly 20 per cent in 1961" (*Report of the Royal Commission on the Economic State and Prospects of Newfoundland and Labrador*, St. John's, 1969:121).

Newfoundland, having become more integrated with the Canadian or North American economy as a whole in the previous decade, and being highly dependent on federal Canadian spending, thus experienced what may be termed a minor depression. Other factors, more specific to the province, added to the crisis.

In the late '50s and the '60s, an extensive mechanization of the logging industry began and is still going on. Whereas in 1956, the number of men taking part in the logging operations had been about 16,000, in 1961, the number dropped to about 9,000 and in 1968, to about 4,200 (see Curran, 1971). This mechanization affected the 'professional' loggers as well as the fishermen-loggers. Some loggers were able to get new employment on the basis of skills they had required in the woods operations, for example, in the use of heavy equipment. Most, however, had no convertible skills and had to rely on the availability of unskilled employment. The loggers who had been hardest hit were those who were regarded as less 'professional': younger loggers with few years in the woods; older loggers past their prime; and people who had not worked in the woods all the time, but had been in and out of logging according to the availability of other work.

The mechanization of the logging industry also eventually made it possible to combine fishing and logging since mechanization involved continuous operations and more full-time loggers. The recession and mechanization resulted in a return to fishing.[7] In 1963, the number of registered inshore fishermen had risen to 20,300 compared to the all-time low of 14,300 in 1956 (Dept. of Fisheries, Economic Service).

The fishermen who went back to fishing were not always the best fisher-

---

7 The items of new technology introduced included the power or chain saw, trucking (substituting horses and river transport), the skidder and the slasher. The chain saw was introduced by the loggers themselves and the other items by the companies. For the cumulative effects of the new technology on manpower reductions as well as work organization, see Curran, 1971 and Peters, 1967.

men. This was so because the most skilled fishermen tended to be the better carpenters, construction workers, and the like. Many men who did return to fishing had to start anew since they had not kept up their equipment. Many had to fish on their own and with the simplest equipment because of the lack of capital and because they hesitated to commit themselves to the fishery on the chance that they might go back to their previous employment when the recession was over. Many were unsuccessful and found themselves without a viable livelihood with the slightest decrease in catches.

Indeed, a general decline occurred in the catches in the inshore cod fishery, largely it seems because of increased trawler fishing by foreign fleets on the fishing banks surrounding Newfoundland. At the same time, the market organization for fish within the province was not developed, a situation partly due to resistance to organized marketing on the part of other Canadian provinces. In most outports, fishermen were not able to market fish other than cod, and other species, making up perhaps 20 per cent of the catch, were thrown back into the sea largely because of the centralization of fresh fish plants. Moreover, fish prices did not rise in spite of the decrease in catches, while the cost of fishing equipment increased.

The loss of income was compensated to some extent by the introduction of unemployment insurance to fishermen on April 1, 1957. While Confederation gave most Newfoundland employees unemployment insurance benefits, fishermen first became entitled to them in 1957 under a special "fishing seasonal benefit." Since most fishermen were self-employed, a special insurance system had to be set up for them.

The device adopted was to measure how much a fisherman worked by the amount of fish deliveries made by him, with contributions being shared by the fishermen and the fish buyer, the latter functioning as employer for the purposes of the scheme. As long as a fisherman made a minimum of fifteen contributions (one for each week of the season in which he made a delivery of fish in excess of a specified minimum), he was entitled to draw benefits without specific proof of his inability to find employment. However, this entitlement started with the first week in December and ended with the week of May 15th. As with the regular unemployment scheme, benefits were reduced or cancelled any week in which the fisherman showed earnings in excess of a stipulated scale (Copes, 1964:16).

The economic recession in the late 1950s and early '60s coincided with the entry into adulthood of those born during the "baby boom" in the early '40s. The effect of the high birth rate on the employment situation in the province has been stressed by the Newfoundland government to the extent that, "If Newfoundland, in the past dozen years or more, had had the average birth rate prevailing across Canada, ... there would perhaps be little or no unemployment in Newfoundland today" (Government of Newfoundland and Labrador, Budget Speech, 29th March 1968:15).

The high birth rate in the province was, however, more than compensated by out-migration to the Canadian mainland. While estimates during the first half of the '50s show a net in-migration to Newfoundland, net out-migration between 1956 and 1961 was about 16,500 and between 1961 and 1966, about 25,000. Gross out-migration of Newfoundlanders was even greater. According to the census of 1961, there were close to 7,500 people from mainland Canada and from abroad residing in Newfoundland who did not reside there in 1956. Gross out-migration of Newfoundlanders during 1956–61 should accordingly have been about 24,000. Statistics for in-migration are not available for the 1961–66 period but with the same ratio, it would add up to about 35,000, and the out-migration seems to have increased rather than decreased in the second half of the '60s. (Personal communication, M. Staveley, Department of Geography, Memorial University.) This means that about 7,000 to 8,000 Newfoundlanders are leaving the province annually and one can easily calculate that this out-migration would affect the employment situation within the province.

While the statistical evidence of the extent of out-migration is scanty, statistics on age, sex, educational level, and occupation of those who leave are even more obscure. However, from limited checks by the author and other persons, the majority of migrants seem to be young unmarried persons, 16 to 30 years of age, of both sexes but with males predominating. Most of the migrants seem to have moved to Ontario, especially to the Toronto area.

The fact that Newfoundlanders leave for the Canadian mainland does not mean that they can all be excluded from the Newfoundland labour market. In fact, many of the new jobs that are created in the province are picked up by migrants who have returned. Even a greater number are planning to, or would like to come back to the province permanently. They are still Newfoundlanders; as one migrant put it, "If there was work in Newfoundland, 50 per cent would go back tomorrow."

For the present theme, namely, the employment situation in Newfoundland, this actual and potential back-migration has both a positive and negative side. On the one hand, the mainland acts as a training ground and may be regarded as a skill pool that can be and indeed already has been functional in the economic development of the province. On the other hand, the large number of mainland Newfoundlanders who want to get back "home" means that more jobs have to be created in the province to keep the unemployment rate at the same level. There is, at present, a growing competition for jobs in the province between mainland and island Newfoundlanders and in this competition, the island Newfoundlanders, especially those presently unemployed, are the most likely losers.

Moreover, the government-institutionalized resettlement programme seems to have created a large number of losers. In many cases, the programme appears to have increased un- and under-employment for a large proportion of the relocatees. In a recent cost-benefit analysis of the scheme (Robb and Robb, 1969), it was reported that approximately one-third of the households found that they had benefited from the move, one-third said they were not worse off nor were they better off, and one-third said that they were worse off.

My primary concern here is with the latter third and with the *non-selective* aspect of the resettlement programme – when whole communities are resettled. The point I want to make is that although a majority of a resettled population might be better off economically and socially, it is highly probable that a large minority of the population will be worse off. This is partly due to the fact that the possibilities for self-employment (notably fishing) and for various kinds of subsistence production are restricted in the reception centres. The relocatees thus become more dependent on the availability of wage work, largely unskilled, which is constantly decreasing. The jobs that are created have a tendency to be more and more specialized, and this means that fewer relocatees qualify for them.

The outport situation had almost the reverse effects. Even in most fishing outports, a substantial group of people get their income from work outside their own community. Their reasons for still residing in the outport are that the work is seasonal, that the place of work is not constant and that they have 'free' housing in the outport, and that the transportation problems are not too great.

The commuter and the local fishermen in such communities might be said to live in a symbiotic relationship. Thus, if the commuters moved, the rest of the population, the fishermen and other local workers, would not be able to maintain proper services such as the school, church, post-office, snow clearance and so on. Resettlement would typically be to a more central location which is usually not the best place for fishing. For the commuters, this would not make too much difference, but for the fishermen it would, unless a new technique for fishing were introduced at the same time, which would make nearness to the fishing grounds a less important asset; long-lining would be such a technique.

The consequences of the resettlement programme on the sector of the population that does not find work in the new centre does not seem to concern the authorities. Government officials argue that the programme has not resulted in higher welfare costs. One reason why this might be so is related to distribution. There may be a smaller number of people receiving welfare in the reception centres, but there is a larger group who have to rely on welfare as their *only* or *major* source of income.[8]

8 The role of the outports in cushioning the effects of unemployment is not a recent phenomenon. "In 1942, 10,000 men were laid off from construction work but this did not create the anticipated unemployment problem since war markets for fish were good and people could go back to the outports" (McKay, 1946:224).

The government seems to be aware of such processes but argues that "even if there is no employment for those who move, their children will be provided with opportunities for obtaining the education necessary to gain employment" (Dr. F. W. Rowe, Minister of Education and sometime Minister of Community and Social Development, as reported in the *Evening Telegram,* October 19, 1967).

There are a number of questionable assumptions in the above statement. While few people would disagree that education should have a high priority in the social and economic development of the province, it might be questioned whether the economic costs of bringing the educational facilities to the people are not less than those of bringing the people to the educational facilities. Even granted that the provision of educational facilities of quality costs less when done under a centralization programme, this saving may well be considered too expensive in view of the social costs it involves. Moving people primarily for educational purposes involves the writing off of a large number of people above school-age if unemployment is their fate. Even if the older generation were willing to accept these costs for the sake of their children, it seems to be an excessive demand to make. Thus, the older outport generation is bearing a disproportionate share of the struggle for the modernization of Newfoundland.

Although it would seem feasible to reduce the number of settlements in the province as a long-term goal, and to canalize an increasing number of people into the urban-industrial sector of the economy, at any point of time there should be a balance between new employment opportunities and resettlement. The problems created by unemployment and welfare in the immediate present might indeed result in insoluble problems in the future.

A concomitant of the high unemployment rate has been the large number of people getting their main income from public welfare or, in official terminology, able-bodied relief. In 1968, more than 17,000 families received this kind of assistance from one to twelve months of the year. Although most of them received relief for a shorter time (40 per cent for three months or less), there has been a steady increase in the number of long-term recipients.[9] This means that a growing sector of the work force is being more or less permanently detached from the economy and is sinking into a 'welfare state.'

* * *

The general socio-economic processes which have characterized the overall Newfoundland scene are reflected at the local community level. I shall concentrate here on one small community which I call Squid Cove.

9 While the number of families receiving able-bodied relief for nine to twelve months in 1964–65 was close to 3,000, in 1967–68 it was over 4,000. For details on welfare statistics see Annual Reports of the Department of Public Welfare 1950–69, St. John's.

Squid Cove was first settled in the latter part of the last century by people mainly from various fishing communities "further out the bay." The first time the community appeared separately in the census (1901), it had a population of seventy.

Their reasons for resettling appear to have been the lack of agricultural and forest resources for subsistence production in their home communities and also increasing employment opportunities in the newly established sawmill industry further inland. Most of the early settlers, however, still took part in the Labrador fishery in the summer months as they had done before they moved. For the rest of the year, they were engaged in woods-work, either as loggers for one of the sawmills in the area or as self-employed men cutting logs for the building of boats and schooners, stages, wharfs, houses; they also made staves and hoops for the fish merchants in the outer fishing communities.

With the decline of the Labrador fishery following a drop in the world markets after World War I, most of the men in Squid Cove and similar communities turned their full attention to the forest. While the first generation of settlers in Squid Cove and other "bay" communities with poor fish resources can be described as fishermen-loggers, the majority of the second generation came to rely on logging as their sole or main source of cash income. The decline of the fishery happily coincided with the establishment of a pulp and paper industry in central Newfoundland.

From the 1920s and for the following three decades, Squid Cove was a typical logging community adapting to the seasonal pattern of supplying pulp for the paper companies described earlier. The population grew slowly and in 1935, it numbered 179; the increase seems to have been due to natural causes. In-migration ceased largely because of poor communications and lack of facilities such as a merchant and a school. Not until after Confederation did Squid Cove acquire a road connection with the island proper; transportation was by dog sled in the winter and by boat and foot the rest of the year.

Other communities in the area with better transportation facilities and better services experienced constant in-migration although the majority of the inhabitants were also dependent on logging. In these other communities, Squid Cove was looked at as a rather poor village.

After Confederation, along with the road connection, Squid Cove also got electricity and telephone service. In addition, Squid Cove became a cross-road community in that both a central high school and a highway depot were built to serve the surrounding area. A merchant established a store to serve the neighbouring communities as well. At present, Squid Cove has a population of almost six hundred. This great increase may be explained by two opposing factors. On the one hand, the new services established in the community created several new opportunities for employment, but they required, to some extent, skilled labour from outside the community. The road connections also made it advantageous for construction workers to settle in the community.

On the other hand, extensive mechanization of the logging industry has put many loggers in Squid Cove out of work, a situation which together with the general slack in employment opportunities in Newfoundland (and the improved facilities in the community), has made many unemployed people stay in Squid Cove rather than move elsewhere. It is difficult to compile clear-cut occupational statistics for the working population in Squid Cove since many men are engaged in several jobs during any year, and many often work at different jobs from one year to the next. It thus seems as appropriate to describe the employment structure in terms of sources of employment as in terms of occupations.

The major source of employment for Squid Cove men is still in logging. Most of the present-day loggers engage in no other work during the year and except for a slack period of a couple of months during the winter and one month during the summer (due to fire hazards), they normally work all year. Some of the loggers, however, stay home for the whole winter drawing unemployment benefits while they work at tasks around the home such as repairing or rebuilding their house, and cutting and hauling firewood. In the spring, some also engage in lobster fishing, especially if the main logging season starts late.

Construction work is the second largest source of employment. Construction workers, largely carpenters, often work for a year locally if such work is available, and in any part of Newfoundland or even Labrador the next year. Also, they may work locally and non-locally during the same year depending on the availability and duration of the construction project. Commonly, they are out of work during the winter months when most construction is impossible because of snow and cold weather conditions. It could be added that the majority of the construction workers are former loggers who, according to their own admission "were lucky to get out of the woods early enough."

A number of men also engage in seasonal non-local fisheries, such as the Labrador and Straits fisheries. During the '50s, the prosecution of the Labrador fishery had almost come to a halt, but started anew in the '60s, with fluctuating results. The last two seasons have been a total failure for most vessels. A few men have also been crew members aboard inshore fishing vessels in communities five to six miles from Squid Cove. These men try to combine fishing with any other work they can obtain, local and non-local.

Whereas men engaged in logging, non-local construction work, and fishing have to stay away from the community for at least a week at a time, the fish plant workers usually commute daily since the plant is only ten miles away. Fish plant work is also seasonal as the plant operates only from late May until November; even during this period, labour demands fluctuate because of unstable supplies of fish. It should be added that the pay for fish plant work is much lower than for either logging or construction work, and it is often difficult to "feed a family" having only one wage-earner.

The majority of men in Squid Cove find employment outside the community, but there are a variety of jobs available within it many of which are year-round. The largest local employers are the highway depot and the central high school which each employ about a dozen people. However, only some of the jobs are held by Squid Cove people. The store owned by the merchant also employs about a dozen persons all year, and it is the only place of work for women in the community. In addition, there are several small saw mills which employ two or three men each, more or less all year since the timber is cut locally in the winter months.

The seasonal sources of employment in the community may be classified according to whether they are permanent or casual. The permanent jobs include fishing which is the major source of income for about six men, a commercial farm employing two or three men in the high season, and a park employing three or four men in the tourist season. Casual jobs are found primarily in various construction projects. Some of these projects may employ a large number of men for a time, for example, in building a new road or a school; government policy requires that the companies involved recruit a certain percentage of the workers from the area in which the construction takes place.

Most Squid Cove men would prefer regular local work to non-local work even if they then had to accept lower wages. Thus one finds that when there is a local construction project, construction workers away on a job often return to pick up the local jobs. As a consequence, men who are un- or underemployed and have greater need for the work, do not get the jobs since those workers who return generally have the higher skills.

Squid Cove men who have insufficient skills to be employed as master craftsmen, but can get employment only as so-called labourers, also find that they "have little to take home" even when they can obtain work outside the community. Earning, say, $1.40 an hour, their weekly wage (at 50 hours) is about $70; having to pay $20 to $30 a week in board and $10 for transportation home on the week-ends as well as social insurance and other expenditures, they may be left with $30 or less – which they could get on welfare. The effort might still be worthwhile economically if the take-home pay were increased by plenty of 'over-time' pay and also if the project were of such duration that it enabled them to qualify for unemployment insurance for the winter months.

However, as the Department of Public Welfare states (Annual Report, 1964:73), "the demand for unskilled help in the various avenues of employment is becoming less each year." Few of the less skilled men seem to have

opportunities for work even outside their own community. The mechanization of the logging industry also reduced that source. The '62–63 Report
states "... the curtailment of logging operations by both paper companies ...
has meant that great numbers of loggers from this district (including Squid
Cove) have been unable to engage in this occupation. Appeals for Public
Assistance, therefore have been relatively high and it is feared will continue."
The '63–64 Report adds that "... the employer can be more selective, re-
jecting those whose previous work records are found to be unfavourable."

At present, of the 120 household heads in Squid Cove, 26 are on able-
bodied relief or welfare as their main or only source of income. But while
the number on welfare has increased drastically in the last few years, some
have been unable to secure any or only casual work since the late 1950s.
Some, because they have had accidents at work, have been able to get long-
term social assistance, or a "medical certificate," as it is called locally.

We can thus distinguish a variety of 'types' of unemployed men in Squid
Cove according to (i) how many years they have been without work, (ii)
what kind of working career they have had before they became unemployed,
and (iii) the extent to which they have to rely on public assistance; that is,
how much employment they have been able to secure even if they have had
public assistance as their main source of income, and (iv) whether they are
on able-bodied relief or have a medical certificate.

In addition, some younger men have never been able to secure more than
casual employment since they left school and thus have no working career
at all. However, among the younger generation, there has been a considerable out-migration from the community, especially in the last decade. Most
have gone to Toronto to find work. Only a few married men have left the
community, and those who leave are typically in their prime and have relatively small families or no children at all. A few left their wives and children
behind and returned home only once or twice a year or stayed home during
the winter months.

Another aspect of this migration is that the individuals who move to the
mainland have close kin or friends already there. The importance of knowing
someone in the city should not be necessary to point out; it is important
economically in facilitating one's finding a job and a place to live, as well
as socially. The implication of this 'move by network' is that migration often
tends to be clustered, first within families, and second, within neighbourhoods and communities.

The detailed dynamics of this migration (and back-migration) need not
concern us here. Three aspects of it are, however, of some significance for
furthering the argument of this study. First, there is the financial support
that kin can give their families back home who are under- or unemployed.
Such support, however, seems to be received only from unmarried children.
Secondly, an unemployed man may often have children and other close rela-

tives on the mainland who are not only employed but also have fairly well-paid jobs. Even if they do not give any economic support to their unemployed kin back home, they will generally, by their mere existence, give social support. Finally, persons with no kin or good friends on the mainland are greatly handicapped in moving there, as are men with large families and those with few skills and little education (as are many of the older men in the community).

A major characteristic of Squid Cove, then, is the many ways by which men make a living. At one extreme is the man who has been living almost exclusively off welfare for several years, and on the other, the one who has succeeded in becoming a construction foreman, both perhaps having worked together as loggers over a period of years.

This difference is characteristic not only of Squid Cove but of many outports. The factors responsible for the increased diversity are largely found in the modernization process Newfoundland has gone through since Confederation, opening up new avenues for employment for some, while at the same time, cutting off old ones for others, but not making residential change for either category especially attractive.

The occupations (including, in this connection, public welfare) have a clear ranking as follows (in descending order): the merchants, doctor, and teachers; skilled construction work and other 'new' occupations; the traditional occupations such as logging and fishing; the more casual labour; and lastly, welfare.

The men holding these various occupations are, however, not necessarily ranked accordingly; other personal factors might be as important to a man's rank within the community. Also, men who have had different occupational careers are often kin, neighbours, or past or present friends and workmates; that is, they belong to each other's network of interpersonal relations. Moreover, except for the top occupational category, to demand any form of deferential behaviour from someone in a lower occupational category is not considered proper according to the community moral order. However, the increasing number of men who are not working for a living has created ambivalence in the moral order of the community. The ambivalence arises not so much from a lack of recognition that many may be in need of assistance when "work is scarce," but rather from the fact that it is extremely difficult to evaluate a man's willingness to work and hence, his "worth." Moreover, the amount of money a man gets from welfare is not always too far from what a man earns from working. A comment often heard in the outports is "there's not much point in workin' when your neighbour does just as well by doin' nothin'." This is the subject of the last chapter.

"I've Had Twenty-Nine Years in the Woods"

George was born in Squid Cove in 1914 and has lived there all his life. His father and two of his father's brothers were among the early settlers of Squid Cove. Like most boys at that time, George started working at an early age. He never got much education, partly because of the poor school situation in the small communities and partly, because he had to work to help his family.

I was never no good at learnin'. I got as far as 'Tom's Dog' at school, not any further. I never learnt to read or write. I was strong and thought of nothin' else than workin'.[1]

When I was 13 year old I joined my father fishin' on the Labrador on one of Brown's schooners. Later in the fall that year we went into the woods (logging for the paper company). I never went fishin' no more. I never liked fishin', but I likes the woods. We made more steady money in the woods – you knew what you were getting – not like fishin'.

With the exception of six or seven seasons on various construction jobs, George spent his whole working career as a logger. The first few years he worked together with his father; later he "buddied up" with his two younger brothers and other men from Squid Cove and other logging communities. During the Depression, "work was often scarce," but being single and a member of his father's household, George looks back on the 1920s and '30s as being "as well off as most around here."

That the economic situation was somewhat relieved in the late '30s may have been a decisive factor for George to decide to "have a family of his own." In 1938, he married a local girl, Elizabeth, whom he had been courting for some time. He was then twenty-four years old and already had more than ten years of working life behind him.

Elizabeth was the oldest in a family of ten. Her father had died at the age of forty-two when she was sixteen. He was also a logger and had had an accident in the woods in which he was hit in his stomach and breast by the shaft of an axe; he got T.B. (tuberculosis) and was taken to the hospital too late. Elizabeth, being the oldest, had to take much of the burden of

1 All quotes, when not otherwise stated, are George's words from dialogues with me or from conversations I overheard. The quotes were not recorded in his presence but as soon as possible afterwards. Most of what is quoted was overheard several times, although often worded slightly differently. 'Tom's Dog' refers to a chapter in the reader used in grade one at the time George went to school.

running the household. In George's words, "She had it tough when she was young. She had to do a man's work, cut wood and everything."

George and Elizabeth settled down in Squid Cove and begot their own family; by the end of the war they already had four children. The war years were particularly good for work in Newfoundland and "good years to start a family." With Confederation in 1949, mother's allowance or family allowance and also unemployment insurance were introduced. These benefits, together with highly stable employment in the logging industry seem to have given George a fair standard of living in spite of his growing family (he had nine children by 1950).

In the early '50s, George managed to build a new house, largely by himself, but with some help from a local carpenter. Besides his own labour, it cost him about nine hundred dollars in material (he cut most of the logs himself) and hired labour. He owed little when the home was finished; in his own words, "When I had this house finished, I owed twenty-five dollars. And I tell you how that was. I had Uncle[2] Ben to do some work on the house, and there were some few things that I still wanted to do, but I had to tell Uncle Ben that I couldn't hire him any more because I didn't have no more money. But he said 'that's okay – you pay me when you get some.' So that's how I owed twenty-five dollars."

According to modern North American standards, his house does not compare; it is a five-room one-storey house measuring no more than 24 by 30 feet. There is no running water or flush toilet; the family has to fetch water from a well about 100 feet from the house and the toilet is "out-door." There is no concrete basement and no brick chimney.

George was able to secure employment in the woods both during the recession and the curtailment of many logging operations, largely it seems, because of his seniority as a logger and his acquaintance with one foreman in particular. However, a work accident during the 1960 season marked the beginning of the end of his career as a logger. In this accident, he strained his back and for a while was unable to perform the heavy logging work.

The following year, George worked for only a short period in the woods. He was able to get some employment with a telephone company clearing brush for the lines – much less demanding work than logging. He appears to have wanted to quit logging for good because of the accident, and also because he was approaching his fiftieth birthday and found that he was "gettin' slower."[3] However, he was not able to secure any permanent employment with the telephone company or elsewhere.

Moreover, the following year, his oldest son Eric dropped out of school

2 In the Newfoundland outports, 'uncle' does not necessarily refer to a real uncle. It is a term used for any elderly man who has the respect of the speaker.
3 The loggers are normally paid according to how much wood they cut. If a man was slow, the less pay he earned.

and wanted to start working. The optimal way, if not the only way both of them could get employed was to "buddy up"; that is, work as partners in the woods. Together, they grossed more than $2,000 that season. The next year, George's second oldest son, Tony, also dropped out of school and joined his father and brother. The three of them together made quite a lot of money according to local standards – between $3,500 and $4,000.

After two seasons of all three working together, George had another accident in which he strained his back again. This time he continued to work until the camp he was working in closed for the summer. But that season became George's last as a logger. In this connection, it should be noted that a logger who has had several accidents in the woods is likely to experience difficulties in being rehired, being regarded by the company as a risk.

In the fall of that year, George went to the local doctor and learned that he had a slipped disc. The doctor recommended rest for a few weeks and told him that he was capable of performing only light work. The doctor did not, however, recommend George for a "medical certificate" which would have given him 'disable-bodied' assistance or long-term social assistance as it is officially termed.

George had to accept able-bodied relief for a few months that year. Although his two boys were still working in the woods and were doing quite well, it seemed that George was reluctant to depend totally on their income.

The first year after he "quit the woods," George did manage, in his own words, to "earn his livin'." First, he began lobster fishing. "When I couldn't go back into the woods I had to make my own job, but I can't make a livin' out of it." Then he got a job as a labourer for about six months at a provincial park that was being built near Squid Cove. This job, together with the lobster fishery, got him enough stamps to qualify for unemployment insurance during the winter months.

However, the next year he got only a few weeks' work at the park and a couple of weeks' work for the local school board doing rough carpentry. For the next two years, he was not able to find any local work and the lobster fishery was a failure. "There are too many people at it that shouldn't be. Everybody is at it – the old age pensioners, the people that get their checks (that is, people on long-term social assistance), and many people that's loggin'. That's kind of takin' the livin' from another man. That's not right." The last three years, George has thus had to depend mainly on able-bodied relief to support himself and his family.

George is now (1970) fifty-six years old. He and his wife Elizabeth, age fifty-one, have thirteen children, a large family even by Newfoundland standards. Only eight of the children are presently part of his household (see Table 1, below). His three oldest daughters are all married; one lives in Toronto and two in neighbouring communities less than ten miles from

TABLE I

Composition of George and Elizabeth's Household 1939–1970

Age of Child \ Year	39	40	41	42	43	44	45	46	47	48	49	50	51	52	53	54	55	56	57	58	59	60	61	62	63	64	65	66	67	68	69	70
Sara	0	1	2	3	4	5	6	7	8	9	10	11	12	13	14	15	*16*	*17*	*18*	*19*	*20*	Married					T	T	T	T	T	T
Nina			0	1	2	3	4	5	6	7	8	9	10	11	12	13	14	15	16	17	*18*	*19*	*20*	Married			T	T	T	T	T	T
Lucy					0	1	2	3	4	5	6	7	8	9	10	11	12	13	14	15	*16*	*17*	*18*	*19*	Married		T	T	T	T	T	T
Eric							0	1	2	3	4	5	6	7	8	9	10	11	12	13	14	15	*16*	*17*	*18*	*19*	*20*	*21*	T	T	U	25
Tony									0	1	2	3	4	5	6	7	8	9	10	11	12	13	14	15	*16*	*17*	*18*	*19*	*20*	*21*	T	T
Janet											0	1	2	3	4	5	6	7	8	9	10	11	12	13	14	15	*16*	*17*	*18*	*19*	*20*	*21*
David													0	1	2	3	4	5	6	7	8	9	10	11	12	13	14	15	*16*	*17*	T	T
John															0	1	2	3	4	5	6	7	8	9	10	11	12	13	14	15	*16*	*17*
Ann																	0	1	2	3	4	5	6	7	8	9	10	11	12	13	14	15
Edward																			0	1	2	3	4	5	6	7	8	9	10	11	12	13
Mary																					0	1	2	3	4	5	6	7	8	9	10	11
Henry																									0	1	2	3	4	5	6	7	8
Irene																										0	1	2	3	4	5	6
Dependents	1	1	2	2	3	3	4	4	5	5	6	6	7	7	8	8	9	9	9	8	9	8	8	8	7	8	8	7	7	7	7	6
Total (including working children living at home)	1	1	2	2	3	3	4	4	5	5	6	6	7	7	8	8	8	10	10	10	11	10	9	9	9	10	10	8	7	8	8	8

Legend: italicized numbers designate child working, but living at home,
T designates child working in Toronto.
U designates that child is unemployed for most of year.

home. Two of his sons are also working in Toronto. Of the children living at home, six go to school, one daughter, Janet (twenty-one), is working at a local store, and his oldest son Eric (twenty-four), has been working as a part-time fisherman and logger the last two years. Both he and one of his married sisters have lived in Toronto.

His many children have become assets rather than drawbacks to George since he became unemployed. Welfare payments are calculated on the basis of need and mainly on the number of dependents in the household. Since George has his own house and the opportunity to get his own firewood for fuel, his relief payments are for food and clothing. Both these payments are supplied by vouchers or "orders," and not in cash;[4] only the food orders are given regularly. According to the present regulations, George is allowed food orders of twenty-five dollars each for himself and his wife, and fifteen dollars for each of his seven dependent children; that is, one hundred and fifty-five dollars per month. However, the fact that his daughter is working and yet is part of his household means that about thirty-five dollars is subtracted from his vouchers, and his monthly food order is thus one hundred and twenty dollars.[5]

While this amount in food orders is George's main source of income when he is not able to find any employment, he has a few other sources of income. Of these, family allowance is the most secure and the largest, amounting to forty-two dollars per month. His children, especially the unmarried sons, also send or give their parents various amounts of cash. After they went to Toronto, they did not seem to do this on a regular basis, but rather at particular times, when they knew that the family had special needs. The other children may also send substantial gifts, especially in the form of clothes for their younger brothers and sisters. Gifts, however, also go the other way. For instance, when George gets "fresh" meat from hunting, his wife sends bottled meat to all her children in Toronto, and when the "big boys" have birthdays, she bakes and sends them rather costly fruit cakes.

George also engages in various subsistence activities: fishing, hunting, and some gardening, and is thus able to supply his household with fresh food or just "fresh" as he calls it. Fishing provides him with cod, caplin, herring, mackerel, trout, and salmon; hunting with rabbit, duck, seabirds, seal, and moose; and gardening with a few barrels of potatoes and some vegetables. Most of these items are to be had only in certain seasons and even then, give

4   In 1970 the Newfoundland Department of Welfare began experiments with paying able-bodied relief in cash in some selected areas, presumably to apply the practice to the whole province if it proved successful.

5   The amount substracted from children working, but who were included in the calculation of able-bodied relief, is 50 per cent of any monthly salary over $105 or an annual income of $1,260. George's daughter's salary being about $170 gross, makes this $35. George's 24 year-old-son is not reckoned to be part of his household since, as a logger, he is working away and has to pay board.

highly varying returns. The activities also involve some expenditures, for example, in gasoline and ammunition; these are not necessarily related to the returns. In the fall, however, hunting and fishing may provide the family with two or three "dinners" a week.

The subsistence activities are functional in other ways. They provide gifts to friends and neighbours and the occasion for "just havin' something to do." These aspects of the subsistence activities will be discussed in later chapters. We are interested at this stage in how much the subsistence activities contribute to the household income. The various sources and estimated income of George's household in 1968 are shown in Table 2.

George often commented that his income was "not too much for a large family to live on," and he was supported in his view by the Canadian authorities, that is by the Economic Council of Canada.[6] However, compared to Newfoundland standards, George and his family are not badly off in spite of the fact that he is unemployed. Although few income studies have been carried out in rural Newfoundland, it seems that total real income averages about $4,500; of this about $2,000 is earned cash income, about $1,000 is income from various transfer payments (notably unemployment insurance and family allowance) and about 1,500 is income in kind, including ownership of house (see Wise, 1964; Faris, 1966; Firestone, 1967; Dyke, 1967; Wadel, 1969; Skolnik and Wadel, 1969).

Of course, a large part of George's income is due to the fact that he has many children. If he had only an average number of dependents, his family allowance would be halved and his food orders almost halved; that is, his income would be reduced by about $750, totalling $3,750.

Yet George has experienced a drastic drop in his income since he became unemployed. As already mentioned, he and his two oldest sons had a combined earned cash income of between $3500 and $4000 in the years preceding his having to go on welfare. The boys, then still in their teens, seem to have contributed a major part of their income to the family purse. At present, what his working children (living at home) might be adding to the family income is subtracted from George's welfare payments. In addition, the children who are of school age (some who might have been working by now have continued longer at school) add to the family expenses, especially with regard to clothing. George would remark, "The children needs nicer

6 The Economic Council of Canada used two cut-off points in establishing the poverty line: first, when 70 per cent or more of the incomes has to be used for food, clothing and shelter. On this basis low-income families are estimated to include families of two with less than $2,500 in annual income and families of three, four, five, or more with incomes of less than $3,000, $3,500, and $4,000 respectively. When 60 per cent of the income is used for food, clothing and shelter, the cut-off points are estimated to be $3,500 for a family of two, $4,000 for families of three and four, and $5,000 for families of five and more (Economic Council of Canada, *Fifth Annual Review*, 1968:108–110).

TABLE 2

Sources and Estimated Amounts of Income 1968

Earned cash income	
Lobster fishing	$ 300
Wage work	$ 200
Total earned cash income	**$ 500**
Other cash income	
Social assistance (in vouchers)	$1200
Family allowance	$ 540
Allowance from daughter	$ 180
Allowance from son	$ 200
Total other cash income	**$2120**
Total cash income	**$2620**
Income in kind	
Fish	$ 260
Potatoes	$ 30
Birds	$ 50
Moose	$ 75
Rabbits	$ 25
Sealmeat	$ 30
Firewood	$ 200
Ownership of house†	$1200
Total income in kind	**$1870**
Total real income	**$4490**

† Rent saved, calculated at $100 per month.

clothes to go to school. They have clothes they could go to church in, but now, they needs nice clothes to go to school in every day." Since George became unemployed, the composition of his household thus carries higher expenditures with fewer income earners to compensate for them (see Table 1).

Still, what has changed most since George became unemployed is not his income compared to other rural households, but rather the source of his income. While the major part of it used to be earned cash income from work (including 'earned' unemployment insurance), his major if not only income at present is able-bodied relief. George's various complaints about the inadequacy of the *amount* he receives seem to be as much complaints about the source. In his own view, he is not only economically but also socially deprived in having to rely on able-bodied relief to provide for his family. He often made comments to this effect: "I was always able to provide for my family (myself). You wouldn't know how bad it feels for a man who has been workin' all his life to have to go to the government."

Welfare or able-bodied relief is looked upon by the public at large, including the outporters, as belonging to a different moral category than unemployment insurance benefits, or for that matter, other transfer payments. Unemployment insurance is "something you work for" and is thus associated with an occupational status; family allowance is associated with taking care of children especially as it applies to large families, 'disable-bodied' assistance with being sick or disabled, and old age pensions with the status of senior citizen. Able-bodied relief, on the other hand, has no such positive association but carries a connotation of disgrace and unwillingness to work.

This is symbolized by the way that able-bodied relief is distributed. Most recipients find the way that it is distributed humiliating. George would remark: "Why can't they give it to you in the mail like they do with other payments. Now you have to line up at the (welfare) office – it's for everyone to see you." The welfare office for the Squid Cove community is only a sub-office and therefore open only on certain days; this makes for greater 'visibility.' The office is, furthermore, situated in another community a couple of miles away and there is no public transport. Therefore, if one could not get a lift,[7] one would have to walk, and in George's words, "a man walkin' that way – people know where he's going." To be on welfare is thus very apparent, a kind of public display. Even though most people in a small community would know who is on welfare anyway, the public display is another matter. In a small community, there are always many unfavourable items of information that people know about one another. However, a considerable amount of such information is talked about only in the family and other back-stage settings. Congenial interaction can occur in other settings as long as people are willing to pretend they do not know and as long as the unfavourable information is not displayed in other ways. The way welfare is distributed makes such discretional devices impossible.

Most welfare recipients also seem to find facing the welfare officer highly embarrassing. Partly because of the criticism, by the media and the public in general, of the great amount of the provincial budget spent on welfare, in 1968, the government instructed the welfare officers "to give closer personal study of each individual case, not merely when the applicant makes his initial application for relief but on each monthly occasion when he renews his application" (Budget Speech, 1968).

To George and others for whom welfare is not just a temporary solution, this "close personal study" must appear unnecessary and highly embarrassing. "First he (the welfare officer) will ask you if you tried to get work before he gives you an order. He will ask you if you made any money or if you will make any in the month. How can you tell him what you're goin' to make in the month to come, when there's no work? He will ask you if

7 In some communities a merchant will often take men to the welfare office in his truck – provided that they cash their order in his store.

there's anyone working in your house. He will ask you what they make in the month to come, and so on."

The uneasiness and, indeed, antagonism which many welfare recipients feel is reinforced by three other factors. First, the federal and provincial governments constantly bring in new regulations with regard to welfare which are not always for the better from the recipients' point of view. Besides, many recipients get little or no information about the changes except when and what they are told by the officer; they often blame the officer for making his own rules, thereby putting him on the defensive.

Secondly, there is a high turn-over of welfare officers because of a high circulation in and out of the service, especially among the younger ones. It seems a deliberate policy of the welfare authorities not to let an officer stay long enough in any one district so as to become too familiar with his clientele and consequently, too lenient. The constant changing of regulations and shifting around of officers seem to be measures of maintaining bureaucratic procedure in the handling of clients.[8]

Thirdly, men such as George seem to find the youth of many of the officers incompatible with their authority. Many of them are in their early twenties and are often university students with no previous work experience. For men with a long working career behind them, the fact that they are being evaluated by "youngsters who's never known what hard work really means" angers them and, indeed, sometimes leads to assaults on an officer. On the other hand, the respect for elders which young men are supposed to show according to outport tradition, is incompatible with their role. Older and more residentially stable officers seem to be able to play a less bureaucratic role better than younger and less stable officers. If an older officer asked the same intimate questions as a younger one, welfare recipients would often excuse the older officer's behaviour saying, for instance, "you can't blame him, he's only doing his job."

For most recipients, it seems to be of great importance that the officers understand why they are on welfare and that the officers are ready to listen to the various excuses they might have. Most excuses, however, are completely irrelevant to the evaluations and decisions the officers have to make. The recipients also want to 'make small talk' with the officer about things not directly related to welfare, if nothing more than about the weather or a local issue. The reasons for wanting to make the interaction more personal are clearly related to the feeling of personal failure attached to the client role of welfare recipient.

The welfare officer, on his side, is often reluctant to be too friendly with the clients, to listen to a recipient's excuses, or engage in small talk for the purpose of helping his clients. Rather, he is supposed to do rehabilita-

8 Gouldner (1954) has found the same process in industry; i.e., how turn-over at the executive level tends to further bureaucratic procedures.

tion work and many officers are heard complaining that they have too few possibilities to do this with men on long-term relief. Rehabilitating the able-bodied implies securing them work first of all, but the officers have no expertise with the labour market and generally can help little in this respect. As one young officer remarked, "able-bodied relief is just to give out money."

Some officers feel that distributing cheques is contrary to rehabilitation, at least with regard to the chronically unemployed. Rehabilitation in their case could mean restricting payments so that they did not become totally dependent on welfare and giving them incentives to get casual jobs and do things for themselves. Being too friendly and lenient with their clients would hinder such an approach, the officers seem to feel. An actual incident may make the strategies involved clearer.

One fall George discovered that there was a leak around one of the windows in his house which caused the panel and floor to rot. He asked the welfare officer for money to buy the materials necessary for the repairs. Funds for house repairs are legitimate items according to the regulations for social assistance. Tells George, "The officer come down to have a look at the house and said: 'George, you have a good house here.' I said, 'Yes, but you can't see what's underneath.' So I showed the welfare officer the leak and he said he'd see what he could do. A few days later he come back and said I'd be allowed to earn thirty dollars for material to repair the house without this changing my order."

George was, in fact, able to earn thirty dollars by doing a couple of painting jobs for his neighbours (one of the two small jobs he had that fall), but he felt humiliated because the welfare officer's suggestion implied that he did not try to earn the money himself, and because he thought he had a *right* to some money to repair the house.

George also seems to feel that he should have been allowed to earn a few dollars without having his welfare payments cut. "I would like to do a few more things (with the house) but I can't afford that. I was able to build this house but now I can't keep it up. The house needs a coat of paint now but that will cost me forty dollars and that means that the family has to do without somethin' else they needs."

The efforts of the welfare officers to rehabilitate by restricting payments also make it more difficult for George to maintain his present standing in the community since that involves, among other things, being able "to keep the house in good shape." An additional reason why George finds his situation especially humiliating is that he is so heavily dependent on relief and earns such a small part of his income himself. Able-bodied relief can be more acceptable to the individual as well as the community if it is relied on for only a short period of the year. Many seasonal labourers and loggers, for instance, do not qualify for unemployment all year, or they do qualify but with lesser benefits than they would get on able-bodied relief. Persons in the latter category can apply to the welfare authorities for what is called supplementary assistance and those in the former category may rely on able-bodied relief for some months of the year. Also, many fishermen who qualify for unemployment insurance benefits from December through April have found it necessary to apply for able-bodied relief in October–November when fishing is poor and before their insurance payments start, and in April–May when the payments cease and the fishery has not yet begun.

The fisherman's reliance on able-bodied relief for a few months of the year is typically due to poor fishing and in any one region, a number of fishermen are likely to find themselves in the same situation. In such cases, public relief may be looked upon by the community as a kind of "catch failure" assistance. However, an increasing number of fishermen have come to rely on able-bodied relief in the fall and spring year after year because of generally decreasing catches and the difficulty of securing any kind of wage labour.

How the community reacts to this use of welfare largely depends on the occupational structure of the community. In occupationally homogeneous communities, for example where logging or fishing predominate, the lack of employment would affect many men and not only a selected few. The more persons finding themselves in the same situation, the more acceptable is the application for assistance. If one man were to go to the welfare officer, he would often start a rush. "If he can do it, I can do it as well," seems to be the reasoning, and the reliance on welfare is thus *synchronized*.

For the individual, it is also more acceptable to live off welfare when one knows it is a temporary solution. One does not need a full year's work to show that one *can* and is *willing* to work. Welfare, in this context, becomes more like unemployment insurance. In inshore fishing, the summer season requires a lot of preparatory work, thus extending the seasonal nature of the fishery into more of a full-time occupation. Fishing may thus be described as a nexus which alleviates deprivation and the feeling of unemployment. The status and acceptability of welfare at the community level is therefore a relative matter, related to the length of time during a year one has to rely on it, and to the extent one's peers have to rely on it.

In spite of the fact that George has been relying on welfare heavily for several years, he has been able to maintain to a large extent his self-esteem and his previous social standing in the community. The main reasons for this seem to be that he has a number of, what might be called 'reserves' of self-esteem to sustain him. The most important of these is a long working career ("I've had twenty-nine years in the woods"). "People that don't know me might look down on me – they might see me around the house not workin'. But the people that know me, they understand. Most people round here know me – they know I been workin' in the woods all my life. Strangers I can tell (that I've been workin' all my life) but they can never be sure, say you, for instance." George still talks a lot about his *past* working life. Indeed, his "career" in the woods is one of his favourite topics of conversation and he often describes in great detail the working process, the area he worked in, the wood camps, the difficulties of getting in and out of the woods, prices for wood in the old days, the policies of the company, whom he worked with, what kind of fellows they were, and many other items. Most of his monologues have a point to them which makes them good stories; in this sense, they may be regarded as pure entertainment or pastimes. Nevertheless, most of the stories end with statements about how many years he worked in the woods, how hard he had to work to provide for his family and the toughness of woodswork in general, and about the fate of loggers:

> I've had twenty-nine years in the woods.
> I worked hard, sometimes too hard.
>
> I worked hard to provide for my family.
> The pay wasn't what they get now.
>
> I guess every logger over fifty is torn down.
> You had to work hard in the woods to keep pace,
> work with a bended back all day long.
>
> Now the company try to get permanent jobs in the
> woods – ten or eleven months. People won't last
> very long with that, it's hard work.

Besides their entertainment value, these stories are important reminders to listeners and to himself about his former occupational status, and they show his willingness to "work for a livin'." George still refers to himself (and is talked about by his friends and neighbours) as a logger. Calling himself a logger seems to indicate not only that he spent most of his time in the woods, but also that he can be identified by a 'profession.' When we occasionally talked about another person who had worked in the woods, sometimes for more than ten years, George would say, "he's not really a logger, he only worked in the woods for a few years."

On a few occasions George argued, always somewhat hesitantly and indirectly, that the paper company for which he had worked so long should have given him a kind of pension:

> Family men workin' in the woods are not able to
> put anything away for a rainy day.
>
> I got a nice paper from the company when I left
> the woods after twenty-nine years, but it's worth
> no money.
>
> There was no kind of pension or that kind of thing
> in the woods – sometimes I think there should have been.

To have a pension would be, George seemed to feel, a very different matter than to be dependent on the welfare authorities. A pension would have been a recognition of his long working career and would have shown a continuity in his life's work; welfare officers take no account of his former work and welfare symbolizes a break with it. The categories by which the welfare bureaucracy defines eligibility are not related to the regular role structure in the social structure. Rather, these categories define people by non-roles, that is by *un*employment (Cloward and Piven, 1968).

Although George's reminiscences over his past working career do not give him a special status in the eyes of the welfare authorities, they do within the local community; we may call his status 'senior citizen.' Lacking a pension, the senior citizen is not, however, officially or financially recognized before he gets an old age pension at the age of sixty-five or seventy;[9] for George, this means at least ten more years of waiting.

There is still another function in George's reminiscences over his past working career. They seem to cultivate the mental attitude of a man *in work* and he could therefore resume work more easily should it become available. His talk about work should be regarded as not only an expression of the fact that he values work but, indeed, as a process maintaining this value.[10] If this view is correct, it can be assumed that once George (and men in similar circumstances) ceases to reminisce over work, or as the subject of work enters less and less into his conversation, then he will have withdrawn more from the labour force and become more unemployable. He may still talk about his past working career but it will be directed only towards making impressions on other people.

The lack of employment opportunities in Newfoundland for men like George would seem to make this latter function more conspicuous.

9   One does not qualify for old age pensions in Canada before the age of 70; however, old age assistance is available at 65.
10   I am grateful to David Alexander of the History Department at Memorial University for drawing my attention to this point.

George's chances of ever getting to "earn his living" or even a modest part of it seem rather bleak. Although he constantly talks about various possibilities and has approached potential local employers in the last few years, his optimism is diminishing.

I knows the place I'm in now and I can't get out of it. It's like sittin' in a rockin' chair, you don't get nowhere.

The paper companies won't take people like myself. I'm too old; I'm not as quick as those young fellers; I'll lag behind. It's the same with a contractor. He's got a job on contract – he wants the quickest men to do the job as quick as possible. He's no place for men like me. The work is too hard for me anyway since I hurt my back.

I'll have a job gettin' other work too. I can do a bit of everything, but I'm not very good at anything. I could do rough carpenter work, but there aren't many of those jobs around and too many want them.

Sometimes I wonder if I could put up a barber shop, a small store, or restaurant down in my garden by the road where I could sell a few things. I've always been cuttin' hair in the woods. People come to me now to have their hair cut from around here. I don't charge anything. Sometimes they pay me and sometimes they do me another favour (in return). I've no trainin', I've just taken to it. I've heard there are some courses where they teach you, but I don't know if I can afford that. I don't know if they'll take me in when I can't read or write. I guess you need a license to put up a business.

George has also been considering going to the mainland.

I would have gone to Toronto if I been able to read and write, but I'm afraid I wouldn't be able to get around when I can't read – understandin' the signs and all that, and I wouldn't be able to write any applications and things like that. I would feel like sinkin' through the ground if somebody asked me to write something and I would have to say that I couldn't. Twice I dreamt that I was in Toronto. The last time I had work too, but I was laid off after two days. I was workin' with a machine where I had to put somethin' into it. But the things were too big to get in, and the foreman came and had to change the whole machine and said, well George, you have to be laid off.

I won't be able to know my way around in Toronto. I would have to have someone to look after me, stay with a family or somethin'. And then I wouldn't be able to take my family all at once. I could maybe leave in the spring and come home about Christmas. I couldn't leave all my family to Elizabeth – she's not strong. I suppose there might be somethin' I could do up there, but it has to be some light work. I'm no good for any hard work no more. And I would have to have at least two dollars an hour to keep my family.

Being dependent on welfare as the major source of income throughout the year and not simply seasonally, is not only depriving but generally makes it more difficult to get into the labour market again. It does so for a number of reasons. First, to get into the labour market again often requires some cash spending especially if one has to go outside the community to look for work. A man who has been on welfare for some time will normally have few cash reserves to engage in such efforts. He is thus handicapped in the competition for work and is likely to be confined to his local area. As one construction worker put it, "You won't get far these days gettin' a job if you don't have a car."

Secondly, having to go on welfare even for a short period often means that one would have difficulties in keeping in touch with potential contacts who could be helpful in supplying work or information about employment opportunities. Jobs in Newfoundland seem to be acquired primarily through personal networks and outport Newfoundlanders do not seem too oriented towards an impersonal job-hunting scheme such as Canada Manpower offers.

Thirdly and closely related to the preceding point, in approaching employers, one must state what employment one has engaged in the previous year; to admit that one has not had any work at all can be very humiliating and even lead to not getting the job. The alternative is deception which often means going around with a constant fear that it might be discovered. In this respect, the man who has been on welfare is in a somewhat comparable situation to the one who has been in jail.

For all these reasons, a man who has been on welfare is often found to show a lack of initiative in looking for a job. When no 'social' initiative is needed, when it is a case of self-employment, welfare recipients show greater initiative. Consequently, many like George, began lobster fishing when they became unemployed, others inshore fishing, and still others cutting firewood for sale. To be able to "make my own job," an investment usually has to be made and therefore, a man is again restricted to his home community.

The opportunities for self-employment are also diminishing, partly as a result of the increase in welfare recipients. The longer one has been on welfare, the more difficult it is to show initiative either in self-employment or in wage-employment. The longer a man has been on welfare, the more he seems forced to adapt to the welfare system and try to get the most out of it.

The restraints on one's being able to show initiative seem to be a major reason why most un- and under-employed Newfoundlanders look to the government and not to private employers for help in getting work. Not being able to show initiative themselves, they have to rely on jobs being *offered* and the government seems to be the only agency capable and willing to make such offers. Private employers always take only the "best," while the government might consider those who need the work most. At least many welfare

recipients think that the government *should* take such factors into considera-
tion; that is, that social as well as economic factors have to be considered.
George would remark, "Why should they (the government through the Department of Highways) always give the jobs on the road to those young
men – some don't even have families. That's work that I could do, and I
need work. Those young can always go away to work."

George also blamed the government for his being without work. "I had
this job in the park, that was work I could do – not too heavy. But why did
the government put me off – there's lots of work to do there still. Why can't
the government let me work for the money and not just give it to me? Now
that's when I wonder if it's cheaper for the government to keep a fellow on
welfare than to give him work. Now, whose fault is that? I'm willin' to work
but there's no work around." While George thus gives the scarcity of work
as the main reason for his unemployment and for being on welfare, he is
well aware that many people think he is on welfare because he is unwilling
to work and does not try hard enough to get work. "People look down on
people on welfare. They think we don't want to work. Now, some of the
things that people said about people on welfare and that "Open Line" programme[1] some time ago – that we are lazy and all kinds of things – that made
me mad. I'll tell you, there are as many good men on welfare as not."

That "there are as many good men on welfare as not" is however a highly
disputed point. One outport merchant expressed a view held by many working men in the outports and elsewhere in this way:

While most people use their brains how to figure out how to *earn* a dollar, other people
(the welfare recipients) use their brains how to figure out how *not* to have to work –
how to beat the rules – and some have become pretty good at that.

The practice of not accepting work when it is available is, according to many,
so widespread that,

... being 'on welfare' has become a full-time profession for a large part of Newfoundland's population. The situation has developed where, in circumstances that are not at
all uncommon, it pays a man more to be out of work than to have a job. We can supply
instances from our personal knowledge of large families with able-bodied men who
have been on welfare continuously for six or seven years without the men even looking
for a job or accepting one if it was offered. ... Something has to be done about such
anomalies. We are not, surely, willing to see a large section of our people relegated
permanently to the status of parasites living on the earnings of their more energetic
or better educated neighbours (*The Evening Telegram*, Editorial, September 28, 1967).

The views expressed here are certainly exaggerated and the provincial
government has found it necessary to repudiate them. In the *Budget Speech*

1 *Open Line* is a daily radio programme in which listeners are invited to phone in and
comment on various topics initiated by either the programme director or the listeners.
Welfare has been a common topic the last few years.

of 1968 the finance minister, after having registered an increasing uneasiness among the populace about the rising costs of public welfare, had this to say:

Mr. Speaker, I think that it is probably true to say that the other large portion of our population that receive welfare payments, the able-bodied, are for the most part honest and deserving citizens who, when they can no longer find work for wages, are forced to apply to the government for enough to keep them and their families going until they do find work. I say that most of them are honest and deserving citizens. But, Sir, there is a minority of whose bona fides we may with some justification have our doubts. The only real cure for able-bodied relief, as we used to call it, is work and wages. If there were jobs for all, then the government would be very wrong to give out a single dollar in able-bodied relief. The government is justified in giving out this kind of welfare only when the people who apply quite honestly cannot find work for wages. When they fail to find work, after a genuine attempt, the government would be very wrong not to give some welfare (p. 55).

A major reason for the dispute about the real cause of unemployment — that is, whether it is due to the unavailability of work or to unwillingness to work – is that it is difficult to measure the availability of work. Each 'authority' is, so to speak, allowed to make his own diagnosis of the 'disease.' When the welfare authorities put a man on welfare, they do not certify that no work is available for the man in question.

Also, the provincial government seems to be somewhat ambivalent about the real causes of welfare. After first having stated that most of the able-bodied recipients are deserving citizens who need help, the finance minister continued:

We have decided, Mr. Speaker, to reduce the scale of welfare payments to all persons on able-bodied relief. We do not, however, propose to reduce the scale of welfare payments to long-term assistance cases such as widows, orphans, sick and crippled persons and other helpless citizens. The new scale that will be paid to able-bodied persons will certainly be less competitive with work rates throughout the province, and we may hope that they will be such as to discourage at least some persons from applying for them (Budget Speech, 1968: 55-6).

Still, there are certainly cases when "it pays a man more to be without work than to have a job" and when some men are not "even looking for a job or accepting one if it was offered." However, the circumstances for such abuses of the system should be stressed. If the work available is local and if it is rejected in favour of welfare, the decision seems to be related to three factors: the wages are too low, not exceeding the minimum wage rate; the work is of too short duration so that going off and on welfare again may indeed mean a reduction in income; or the work is too heavy for a man physically handicapped in some way (see next chapter); or a combination of these three factors. It is highly unlikely that a fit able-bodied man would prefer welfare to a local job paying a fair wage, say $1.25 an hour, and lasting long enough to enable him to qualify for unemployment insurance. I was not able to record any such cases.

On the other hand, non-local work, even at $1.25 an hour, may leave little take-home pay if there is not ample opportunity for "over-time" and/or if it is of insufficient duration to qualify for unemployment insurance. Moreover, considering that most welfare recipients do not possess special skills and that the demand for unskilled workers is constantly diminishing, the opportunities for many welfare recipients to get such work seem difficult.

But even if people agree that work is not available, they still look at welfare as somewhat illegitimate. There are a number of ways in which people tend to explain away the fact that work is not available is the *only* reason why men end up on welfare. First, of course the fact that work is not available does not necessarily ruin the argument that welfare recipients are unwilling to work; unwillingness to work may well be hidden behind an argument that work is not available. This is again related to the belief that work is regarded as somewhat unpleasant; "many people would not work if they didn't have to" seems to be a generally accepted axiom.

A type of observation that seems to lead many people to be sceptical about the motives of welfare recipients is that welfare recipients generally belong to the lowest rung of the socio-economic ladder even if they worked before. They are the first to become unemployed because they have the least education, the fewest skills, the least aggression and initiative, the fewest connections, and so on.

All these concomitants reinforce the negative image attributed to recipients because of their being on welfare. One cannot be sure, and perhaps one would like to believe that their situation is due to their lack of character rather than to the failure of the economy to provide enough employment. In addition, even if able-bodied relief is a statute, it is not regarded as a civil *right* due those who cannot find employment. Rather, it is thought of as something "we," the taxpayers, give to "them," the unemployed. There is no generally accepted feeling that it is the responsibility of the government or the society to secure work; finding a job is primarily the responsibility of the individual himself.

For a welfare recipient to say outright that if work is not available, it is only proper for the government to provide adequate assistance, is not approved. Recipients thus have to be careful not to talk about their "rights" except to other people in the same position. George, for instance, would remark, "When a man has a big family like me, you have to get money from somewhere, and when you can't get no work around, you have to take money from where you can get it." His large family is used to legitimize his "rights." On the other hand, if a recipient does not complain at all, this might be taken as a sign that he is satisfied with being on welfare, that he, in fact, is unwilling to work. Whatever the recipient does, complain or not, he is likely to be sanctioned. Talk about welfare payments between recipients and non-recipients is thus a delicate subject, but one which is hard to avoid.

One basic reason for outport people being resentful of welfare recipients is the low income level in the outports. This is brought out by the fact that the better-off in the outports are often the first to excuse them, at least in private. As one construction foreman told me, "I can't blame them to be on welfare when there's no work around and I don't blame a man who won't go away to work if he only gets the minimum wage and when he has his family and house here. And what they get on welfare, they must have to keep their families. I don't envy them." I doubt that this man would be as outright when talking to his unskilled labourers who do not earn much above the minimum wage.

Many working people who do not have high incomes often complain that, "There's soon not much difference between what a workin' man gets and what one can get on welfare," or "There's not much point in workin' when your neighbour does just as well on welfare."

Welfare recipients are unlikely to get any support from ordinary working people in the community in their insisting on their "rights" or in complaining about the inadequacy of welfare payments. If a recipient does complain, it is likely to be taken as a sign of the lack of modesty. One area, especially, in which it is felt that welfare recipients show no modesty is in their consumption habits. "Those people (on welfare) have everything – T.V., washer, oil stove – everything. There's not much difference between what a workin' man has and what they have. Well, some don't have too decent houses – they don't seem to care too much about that. But inside their houses they have as much as I have."

Criticisms such as the above become more meaningful when one considers that in recent years, outport people have come to measure their 'progress' by the possession of such items as television sets, oil stoves, fridges, and the like. A common explanation for recipients' being able to acquire these modern conveniences is not only that welfare payments are relatively high, but also that recipients abuse the welfare system. Abuses definitely take place and are executed in a variety of ways, some illegal and some legal.

The illegal abuses most often take the form of drawing welfare payments and working at the same time, or of not reporting income from earnings, especially from casual jobs. People who work regularly and still draw welfare seem to be few and it is not something that can be done over a long period without being discovered and brought to the attention of the authorities. On the other hand, not reporting earnings from odd jobs occurs frequently both because the authorities have great difficulty in controlling this practice and because one could easily "forget" to report. It is probable that by abusing the system, a welfare recipient is able to keep up *his* morale (rather than let it break down) in that it acts to maintain a feeling of independence, of not being completely trapped in the welfare system.

Legal abuses of the welfare system can take many forms. An hypothetical case illustrates one way: Say that a man got his food order of $155 for his wife and seven children at the beginning of the month. Later that month, he picked up a job for two weeks and made $100. He used his order and spent the $100 on various things the family needed. At the beginning of the following month, he had no money left (an absolute requirement to get any relief) and asked the welfare officer for a food order for that month. The welfare officer inquired about his earnings last month, as his eligibility depended on his not earning above a net ceiling which for a nine-person household is $255. With his earnings of $100 and his order of $155, this man just reached the ceiling. Therefore, the welfare officer could predict his earnings in the sense of calculating that he would earn $100 the following month also and give the man $55 instead of $155 for his food order. But if the man did not earn anything that month, he would be refunded the difference. The 'good' recipient is supposed to spend the $100 he earned on food and clothing and not come back to the welfare officer before he used it all up.

The extent of the abuse seems to be greatly exaggerated. With regard to the prestige items mentioned earlier, there are several ways welfare recipients can acquire them without stooping to illicit means *vis-à-vis* the welfare system. First, they do so by reducing their 'consumption' of other things, and notably by cutting down on visiting and partying. Second, adult children may have brought a few items into the home. The provincial government, which should be in a position to have an overview of abuses from the many welfare officers, has found it necessary to repudiate many of the complaints.

... nothing is easier than to allow bitter resentment towards those unfortunate persons among us who, having lost their chance to earn an honest dollar, are driven to apply to the people, through the government, for relief. Outrageous stories of laziness, of conniving, of double dealing, and other nefarious practices are circulated from month to month throughout the province, each individual case of malpractice being made to do duty many times over. It is not necessary, and it most certainly is not sensible, for a person unthinkingly and carelessly to accept all these outrageous and exaggerated accounts, but at the same time it is very clearly the government's duty to see that none but the deserving receive welfare from public funds. (Budget Speech, 1968:54–58).

It seems likely that such gossip would function as a deterrent against abusing the welfare system. The welfare officer, himself, would probably be influenced by the gossip since he often has to socialize with local people in order not to isolate himself completely from the community. Also, any welfare recipient wanting to maintain relations with the working people in his community would feel constrained in abusing the system, knowing that he would reap strong disapproval and be the object of gossip.

On the other hand, the mere fact that gossip about abuses is circulating tends to make the character or morality of any welfare recipient suspect.

Anyone wanting to clear himself completely of suspicion would have to be cautious about his consumption habits. He would also have to be careful not to be too intimate with other recipients who are the object of suspicion in the community. Yet, even if welfare recipients observe these unwritten rules, they are not immune from being imputed with other motives for being on welfare than the non-availability of work.

Several welfare officers remarked upon a gradual change in behaviour they observed among their clients. "The first time they come to the office, they may be shy; they look down and talk quietly, on the whole, looking ashamed. However, after some time, they don't seem to mind at all; they even argue and demand. Eventually, the people who are continually on able-bodied relief think that the government *owes* them a living." Such a change in behaviour is typically interpreted by the officers as a change in "character." Remarks such as "they seem to have lost their independence" and "they have no pride left" are commonly applied to long-term recipients.

Although a change in character may definitely occur, especially if a man has been on welfare for a long time, an alternative explanation would be that many recipients become more demanding when they feel they have fewer and fewer possibilities to ever get satisfactory employment. Their demands also increase as they have to replace or repair some of their capital items such as their house, household equipment, and clothing. In such a situation, one can appreciate their having to adapt to the welfare system and trying to "get the most out of it."

The inability to show much initiative and the corresponding adaptation to the welfare system are, by most people, not related to the initial difficulty of getting work. Rather, the lack of initiative is taken to be the *cause* of men going on welfare in the first place and not the *result* of being on welfare. In this way, being on welfare is considered to be due to individual moral deficiency rather than to a structural deficiency; that is, that work is not available for everybody. Such reasoning is most often heard about individuals who have been without work and on welfare for some time. The fact that some of these people have had long working careers before going on welfare tends to be forgotten or at least, undercommunicated.

George's *present* circumstances are, on the whole, acceptable to most local people and one would think to the editorial writer quoted above. Apparently, he has not abused the welfare system in any way, he has a large family to take care of, he has a long working career behind him and one can easily appreciate his difficulties in getting work. All these factors render George a "deserving" welfare recipient. On the other hand, having been unemployed for several years and having few possibilities of getting to earn his living in the future, even his long working career does not make him unaware that he has a vulnerable status. The longer he stays on welfare, the more likely is his "character" to be questioned.

We may compare the status of the chronically unemployed man being dependent on able-bodied relief to the status of the disable-bodied, the man who has been incapacitated from working because of an injury. The disabled who applies for a pension is, in the first place, certified by a doctor or another health authority to be incapacitated. Moreover, he need not base his status on a past working career, but can ascribe his incapacity to a work injury. He can relate to the general social structure in two ways both of which usually have positive connotations.

For these reasons, it seems socially more acceptable to be disabled than chronically unemployed. George is, in fact, declared "unable to do heavy work" by the local doctor because of his back injury. He is not, however, on a medical certificate; that is, declared unfit to do any kind of work and eligible for so-called long-term social assistance or, what I have called, a disable-bodied pension. Such a pension would bring George a monthly allowance of about three hundred dollars and it would be paid by check, eliminating the monthly 'exhibitions' at the welfare office. George and other partially disabled men thus seem to be in a dilemma in having to prove their willingness to work and their eligibility for a medical certificate at the same time.

George talks a lot about his diminishing strength and health. In most conversations with me as well as with other people, he would bring up the question of health in one way or another. But instead of talking about himself directly, he usually brought the conversation around to health in general, or the health of elderly loggers: "I guess every logger over fifty is torn down. Now take Peter down here ..."

He also made predictions about what would happen to the men who were working in the woods at present. "The family men workin' in the woods will end up like me, you know. It's hard work, you don't last too long." The various work injuries he had received, or nearly had, would be described in great detail especially for people whom he had not told the stories to before or thought he had not: of how and where they happened, how he felt, which people witnessed them, what the doctor said, and so on.

It appears that the back trouble George acquired during his last season as a logger has improved somewhat over the years, presumably because he did not go back into the woods and because the work he engaged in since then has been more casual and less harmful to his back. However, George still complains about more or less regular pains in his back, legs, and neck. Occasionally, he has more painful attacks or "spells" as he calls them. "Sometimes it's so bad I can't move. I've had to sleep on the floor and I've even had to stand to eat – couldn't sit down"; or "Sometimes my legs just give in and I can't move. When I have those spells, I can't do anything."

During the fall of 1968, George had at least four spells when he complained about particularly painful aches in his back and legs. The spells did not follow immediately after hard work as one might have expected. Indeed, the times when he was doing fairly hard work, for example, cutting firewood, repairing his house, or moose hunting, he never had any of his spells, although he often complained that he "could feel it in his back." Rather, his spells occurred when he had little or nothing to occupy himself with and always at the beginning or the middle of the week. The spells would last three or four days and then he would feel better over the weekend. There may well have been purely physiological reasons for the occurrence and timing of these spells; I am not in a position to know. However, it seemed that his spells were at least partly determined by social and psychological factors. George's spirit seemed to be at a low ebb during his spells and it seemed to precede rather than succeed them. During these periods, he often complained that he felt lonely and had nothing to do. He also complained that he had lost his nerve and worried a lot.

I worries a lot. Perhaps I always been like that. If I was on my last sack of flour I always worried where I would get the next one from. Sometimes I lie awake all night. Not everybody is like that, some people never worry.

I've lost my nerve. A few years ago I wouldn't mind going in the woods or go fishin' or huntin' on my own. Now I want someone to go with me. I might have a spell – then I wouldn't be able to help myself.

George never called on the doctor when he had his spells or talked to the doctor about his worries although the doctor lived less than half a mile away and passed George's house several times every day on his way to visit patients. He would, however, see the doctor occasionally for other reasons: he used to get bad coughs during the winter (which also gave him the pains in his back) and needed some cough mixture; he was also the one to see the doctor on behalf of his family and to get various medications for them. On such occasions, he and the doctor might exchange a few remarks about George's back pains but it would be left at that. Both the doctor and George thus seemed to avoid the real issues; that is, whether George was sick enough to be liable for a medical certificate or not. I shall discuss the doctor's reasons for avoiding this issue later and concentrate on George at this point.

First, George seemed to think that the doctor knew his situation and that accordingly, there was no need for him to remind the doctor of his trouble. If he tried to remind the doctor, he would do so in an indirect manner as he would do when talking about his health or his working career to his friends and neighbours. When the doctor did not respond to his hints, George seemed to take this as something personal from the doctor's side. "He (the doctor) knows all about me. I don't think he is too interested in me."

Secondly, George regarded the doctor's diagnosis as rather inconsistent: "The doctor tells me that I can only do light work, but there's no light work around here. Now, what do you think about that?" What George might be arguing is that the definition of "incapacitated" ought to be related to the state of the labour market; that is, if he is capable of doing only light work and there is no light work available, he is, in fact, incapacitated. Such a principle has indeed been accepted by the Workmen's Compensation Board. A man who is injured at work to the extent that he is not capable of performing *his* job, qualifies for compensation even if his injury did not incapacitate him from holding *other* jobs. If the injury is permanent, the man is offered assistance for training for another job. There are retraining centres in Newfoundland but George would not qualify, having too little education to start with. Besides, with the present employment situation in Newfoundland, retraining would hardly be enough to secure a job. Being partially handicapped by having next to no skills and in a situation where the rate of unemployment is high seem to add up to being totally incapacitated.

Being partly incapacitated may even involve difficulties in accepting 'light' work as the following incident illustrates. Some time after George had been told by the doctor that he should not engage in any heavy work, several local construction jobs became available and they did not seem to be too heavy. George was somewhat reluctant to apply for one of the jobs but finally did, mainly because the work would last long enough to qualify him for unemployment insurance. Also, the doctor had encouraged him to take any work he felt capable of doing. During the project, however, George "stretched" his back in performing a rather trivial task; it became so bad that he had to be carried home. In George's own words: "I got one of those spells when I can't move. After they got me home the doctor came down to the house. He told me to rest for a week and said I should ask the foreman to put me on the lightest work he could find. I told him (the doctor) 'You tell the foreman that, it's better you tell him.' "

The doctor did not follow George's request to tell the foreman, wanting to "allow him to stand on his own feet" and perhaps not being aware of the reasons George had asked him to be a go-between. George's reasons were related to the difficulty which partially incapacitated men have in defining a protected role in a work situation, themselves, and thus would like to have it defined for them. This is particularly the case when the tasks in the job are not, or cannot be, rigidly defined.

Even if the job one is assigned to is not heavy generally, it may often involve heavy tasks. It would appear "foolish" and "unmanly" to ask a fellow worker or the foreman to give a hand at a trivial task, a task in which, however, an incapacitated man feels he could strain himself. Also, an incapacitated man would have great difficulty in refusing to give a hand if a fellow worker were performing a heavy task. Most men would make an effort to manage the job themselves or give a hand, even if they felt that they took a chance straining themselves. The cost of not helping may be that one is characterized as "tryin' to put all the heavy work on your buddies" and/or "pretending to be more sick than you really are"; that is, one may lose the respect and sympathy of one's fellow workers and superiors.

On the other hand, if a man manages to perform the heavy tasks, he will likely become suspect. The partially incapacitated are thus caught in a dilemma; whatever they do can be interpreted to their disadvantage. Being confronted with suspicion would be humiliating and the anticipation of such situations seems to make men such as George reluctant to take on jobs which are not clearly defined and jobs where they have reason to distrust their fellow workers.

In sum, the fundamental dilemma lies in the "in-between" nature of the illness or handicap of men such as George. On the one hand, if George's health were slightly worse, he would probably qualify for a medical certificate with its economic and probable social benefits. On the other hand, since he is not sick enough, he should be – and is in fact – looking for work. However, getting a job or trying to get a job is the same thing as saying that he is not incapacitated enough to qualify for a medical certificate.

The local doctor, and presumably other doctors with some knowledge of the local situation, recognize the dilemma of these men. Still, doctors find it difficult issuing medical certificates without obvious medical reasons for doing so. For a doctor to include social considerations in his diagnosis, that is, that there is no light work available and that the man is not capable of doing heavy work, lies outside his profession. On the other hand, some doctors include social considerations for *not* giving medical certificates to such men. To start with, one doctor seems to have in mind what may be called the "domino theory": if he gives a medical certificate on social grounds to one man, his doing so might precipitate a rush of men in similar situations. In his words,

> Most men over fifty around here are broken up. One expects a bad back on a logger who's been working in the woods all his life. And most of them also have great difficulties in getting sufficient employment.
> Every time I have a man over fifty or so coming into the office, I expect him to apply for a medical certificate and I'm relieved when it's for a bad toe or something.
> The more people one puts on a medical certificate, the more the will to work for the rest of the community is going to be sapped. One can't just look at the individual case; one has to consider the community also.

The bad backs are a common phenomenon among loggers. This is not surprising considering the heavy strain on the back that especially old-time logging jobs inflicted. Moreover, most of the loggers started working in the woods at an early age in the past, often at thirteen or fourteen; in recent years, they begin at about sixteen. Many of the young men also complain about strained backs; George's oldest son, aged twenty-four, feels back pains sometimes and remarks, "I guess I started in the woods too early."

Bad backs and bad hearts are common complaints among many outport fishermen, also. Although fishing is not generally as rigorous as logging, many fishermen work up to sixteen hours a day during the high season. Most of the older fishermen also started working "as a man" at an early age, and many have also been seasonal loggers (cf. Ch. 1).

But even if there are definite occupational reasons for many outporters' being physically run-down by middle-age, there is also a definite co-relation between unemployment and complaints about a bad back or bad heart which can, at the same time, be interpreted as malingering. For a man who has not been working regularly and who has difficulties getting a permanent and fairly well-paid job, it is clearly convenient to be declared incapable of working: economically, since he would likely have a higher income from being on a medical certificate than from doing casual work, and socially, since it would legitimize the fact that he is not working.

It is obviously easier for a doctor to give a medical certificate to a man who has been working regularly or has a permanent job, than to a man who has been only casually employed. Indeed, the fact that a man who has been working regularly at a fairly well-paid job comes to the doctor, is likely to be taken as medical evidence of his ill health for, as the doctor stated, "one always makes the assumption that a man with a permanent job wants to keep his job."

A second 'social' reason why a doctor feels reluctant to issue medical certificates is that for every person whom he exempts from work without obvious medical reasons, this tends to set in motion a kind of back-lash; men who are "working for a living" get more and more irritated. Many of them are not in the best of health themselves and are working under great strain. They differ from the men described above in that they are equipped with greater skills and therefore, have permanent and better-paid jobs. It is generally the opinion of these employed people which the doctor values most, and they are the people with whom he interacts socially. The doctor thus finds himself under social pressure to be tough about the issuing of medical certificates. I often heard such people complain that the doctor was sometimes too lenient and that he "rewarded people who had never done very much work" and "who were not very sick."

What makes the working men especially resentful of men with medical certificates is the relatively large amount of assistance they get. Long-term social assistance is paid in cash and at the rate of $85 a month for a single person, $130 for two persons and $25 for every additional person. A family with seven children, therefore, gets $305 a month, or more than $3600 a year. Although a man with a skilled job, a carpenter, for example, would have a higher monthly income, say $400, the fact that he is able to secure employment for only eight out of twelve months a year often gives him a lower annual income.

In addition, a man with a medical certificate is allowed to earn $90 a month or $1,110 a year besides his social assistance. If he were able to do this (few seem to be able to) and engage in some subsistence production (which most do), as well as have no rent to pay, he could have a *real* annual income of about $6,000. Although few men with medical certificates seem to have such a high income, some do. One man who lost his right hand working in a sawmill got a medical certificate a few years ago. He has several small children and thus gets a monthly assistance of close to $300. He has a car and uses it to provide a taxi service; he is also a car mechanic and does repair work. Together these jobs presumably bring him the additional $90 per month he is allowed to earn. This man is not only better off than most unskilled workers, but also better off than many skilled workers. He seems to cause a lot of resentment among local people, moreso than men who live largely or solely on able-bodied relief. However, the larger consumption power this man has compensates to some extent for the resentment he experiences by the local community.

While George and other men in his situation think that they would be much better off economically and socially with a medical certificate, the men who actually have one are not free from worries. Besides being considered by the community as recipients of too much money, they have other problems. First, since their sickness is not only a function of health but also of the difficulties of getting employment, they are often tempted to stay sick. Being sick is the most rational way to gain some kind of economic security, as well as make the fact that they are not working more acceptable to themselves and others. Thus, men with medical certificates who cannot get employment often go to the doctor not to seek help, but rather to be reassured that they are still sick. That the doctor adopts an optimistic attitude towards their sickness is discouraging to them. This attitude can be seen most clearly in the trauma which many people experience when they "are taken off" their medical certificate. As the local doctor explained: "The hardest thing in the world is taking somebody (who cannot get work) off a medical certificate. I try to give signals for a long while before I actually do it to make it easier for them."

Secondly, the persons on a medical certificate have to maintain their sick role *vis-à-vis* the community as well as the doctor. The fact that many of them have somewhat invisible illnesses such as a bad back or a bad heart, and that they are not totally incapable of working but can do light work, make it less obvious to the layman that they are "really" sick. Laymen are often heard to dispute the doctor's diagnosis. "I knows a man down here, he's on a medical certificate and I've seen him carry heavy loads of wood on his back all winter. Now he's got himself a horse and goes into the woods with him all the time. He isn't sick ... It's easy to be turned down by the doctor and if the doctor says you are sick, that's it. No one can tell the doctor anything."

The dilemma for the disabled is reinforced by the fact that the doctor encourages many of them to do as much work as they can and to the extent that they feel capable. He does so on medical grounds (exercise is good for heart patients) as well as on psychological grounds – to discourage a man from being totally caught up by his illness. However, following the doctor's advice often results in "talk" in the community and in more severe consequences. To illustrate with a few examples, one man who was on a medical certificate because of a bad heart went lobster fishing in the spring, being encouraged to do so by the doctor. People in the community started to talk about this: that he wasn't very sick and that he took a living from other people. A few days later, the man had a severe heart attack. Another man who had been crippled started to make handicrafts which he sold locally. Some neighbours started to say that he was not allowed to do this.

The man became upset and called the doctor to ask him if he could continue to sell his handicrafts. The satisfaction he got from finding "something he could do" had been taken away from him.

In general, men who get medical certificates seem to want their role-activities mapped out in detail by the doctor. They thus tend to become clients in more ways than one. The doctor of course has difficulties in advising these men on every detail. In addition, he is reluctant to make them more dependent on himself than they already are, both for medical and social reasons. On the other hand, without the 'protection' of the doctor, many men on medical certificates tend to withdraw from social interaction outside the family circle; the local doctor learned that a number of men did not like to go out of their house at all and others stayed around the house most of the time. A consequence of this was that they got restless and more concerned with their health, and in fact, got worse.

Some men have been able to avoid getting into such a situation by performing a service to the community. One man with a bad heart who had been a logger-fisherman for most of his life, began cutting hair and insisted on not charging anything. Largely because of this role, he seemed to maintain his social network in the community. He also keeps a large vegetable garden together with his wife and gives away a lot.

So far, we have considered only men on medical certificates. Although it is much less common, married women can also receive a medical certificate when they are incapable of maintaining their household and, as a result, need their husbands to stay home; in other words, a housewife is not put on a medical certificate directly but indirectly, through their husbands who had to quit their jobs to take care of the household. Such instances where a fit husband stays home because his wife is sick tend to be looked upon by the community with great suspicion, especially if they continue over some time. Even if the wife is known to have a long-term and heavily incapacitating illness, the husband who stays home is often regarded as "hiding behind his woman." Such a view is of course even more common if it is known that the wife is capable of performing *some* of her household duties. In addition, if the husband is known not to be a "hard worker," his reputation is definitely settled.

A husband with a handicapped wife is thus forced into making an arrangement which makes it possible for him to stay at work, if he cares about his reputation. The most common arrangement is to let the older girls take over the household duties or, in the families with only small children, a female relative.

A man who has to stay home because his wife has become incapable of performing her household duties may have difficulty getting back into the labour market, especially if he has few skills. In one case I observed, the wife of a logger had a nervous breakdown and was declared by the doctor "incapable of maintaining household; needs presence of husband probably for at least six months." In fact, she did not get well for over a year and her husband stayed home all the time. He did not keep up his union payments during this time and was for that reason and presumably also because he had not been a regular logger (he used the woods only when he could not work as a carpenter), unable to obtain work as a logger when she did recover. The following year, this man was able to get only casual employment and had to rely on able-bodied relief to support himself and his family. In such circumstances, it would have been tempting for the wife to stay sick and, in fact, the wife in question did not fully recover her health although she is no longer on a medical certificate. The local doctor told me that he expected another nervous breakdown partly because her husband was not able to get a job. The relationship between the spouses might easily become strained in situations where the wife falls ill.

Generally then, it is less problematic for the husband to qualify for a medical certificate. There are at least two reasons for this: first, there is no pressure on an outport wife to become the provider if her husband falls ill, mainly because there is in fact no work for women in an outport. Secondly, as has been shown, a family can be as well off economically with the husband getting a 'disable-bodied pension' as it would be if he were working. It should not be necessary to mention that a decrease in income can be a strain on the husband-wife relationship. It should be expected that a wife, other things being equal, would prefer to have her husband on a medical certificate rather than on able-bodied relief. It appears that it was this difference which led one housewife to say, "My husband is sick and he is going to stay sick as long as I'm married to him."

However, even the wives of men who are on able-bodied relief do not, in general, seem to disparage and feel disparaged by their husbands, and husband-wife relations in many outport welfare families appear to be cordial. This was very striking in the case of Elizabeth and George; one could explain their good relationship by the facts of their long marriage and their personalities. But on the other hand, there seems to be a number of more specific *social* factors involved. If one were to summarize them under a single heading, the clue would be the separation of husband/wife roles in the outports and as a consequence, the separate system of evaluation. That a man has to go on able-bodied relief need not necessarily affect the reputation of his wife as long as she continues to perform *her* role satisfactorily.

George talks very highly about his wife Elizabeth. "I've a good woman and that's been a great help. Not everybody can say that." There are at least two implications in this statement: first, that she is respected by other people in the community and second, that she respects and supports George in his role. My wife and I never heard a person in the neighbourhood or the community say anything negative about Elizabeth. This is perhaps not surprising considering the style of conversation in the outports and also our position as strangers in the community (see Appendix). However, the comments about her were positive; and if she had been disapproved of, there would have been no comments at all, in keeping with the style. Most remarks referred to her being "a good worker"; "she keeps the house nice and clean"; and "the children are all nice." George is very proud of his wife as a home-maker.

She's a hard worker. She's always been like that. Her father died when she was only sixteen and she was the oldest so she had to help her mother. There were many children in the family and she had to do everything, go in the woods and cut wood – everything. She's had it tough.

When I was workin' in the woods she had to take care of all the children and get wood and water; she never complained. She got good help from the children though, when they grew up.

Elizabeth's daily working routine consists largely of preparing breakfast, making the beds, cleaning the house, making dinner, washing the dishes, making supper and finally the night meal, locally called "lunch." Every other day, she bakes bread or washes clothes. Both of these tasks take most of the morning and she tries to arrange it so that she does not have to do both the same day. Every Saturday, she "washes the house" and " changes the beds." During and in between these chores, she attends to the various needs of her seven children still at home, as well as to those of many of their friends.

For the last twenty years, Elizabeth has had a large number of children to take care of (cf. Table I in Ch. 2), the maximum number of ten in the late '50s and the early '60s. She is now over fifty years old, and the many childbirths and hard work have broken her health somewhat. But she is still able to have all her household duties done by adopting special management techniques.

One basic way of managing large families is to let the children take care of one other. The older ones, especially the girls, act in the capacity of mother's helpers. Elizabeth often talked about the help she received from her daughters. At present, Ann has the role of mother's helper. "I don't know what I would do if it wasn't for Ann. She's a great help. I need never tell her what to do. She does things without me sayin' anything."

In this connection, it is interesting to note how much Ann does in the house compared with her younger sister Mary. The latter is characterized by her parents as "very lazy," not helping with anything in the house. She is constantly contrasted with Ann and the difference is explained by the parents in terms of personality. However, another reason might be that the niche of mother's helper is already occupied and there is no room for two. A test of this interpretation was supplied when Ann had to take care of her sister's two children while the mother was away in St. John's. During her absence, Mary was very helpful in the house and received much praise from her parents. When my wife asked Mary and her cousin who was in the same situation (that is, had an older sister who was mother's helper) why they did not help like that all the time, they answered that they (the older sisters) "always criticized their work," and that was why they never wanted to do anything. It should be added that Mary looked after her younger brother and sister, but this work is not as visible to George and Elizabeth as Ann's work in the house.

In spite of the help Elizabeth receives from the older children and Ann in particular, she seems to have more work with seven children than she had with ten. She often complained that she did not have as much time to do things in the evenings, such as knitting and sewing, because the two smallest children require so much attention. This might be because the two youngest have been "babies" much longer than the rest, having no younger brothers or sisters. A second technique in the management of large families, then, is giving less attention to successive children when a new baby is born. The two youngest now have no competitors for their mother's attention and tend to get spoiled. That the above is so seems implicit in Elizabeth's statement: "None of my children has been very good when they were small but they always became better when they got a little older. But Henry and Irene ..."

In addition, Elizabeth is older and not in the best of health, and therefore feels the strain of the children more than she used to. Sometimes she would say "I can't help thinking how easy it would have been if Ann had been the last one."

Elizabeth does not only have her own children to attend to; all her children, especially the younger ones, bring their friends to the house many times a day. Farley Mowat's (1968) vivid description from Newfoundland's South Coast is applicable also to Squid Cove:

The children share a universal family (in the outport). Almost every man and woman of middle age or more in the settlement is honorary aunt and uncle to every girl and boy. Each home is nearly as much the home of every child as is the one wherein he or she was born. The children circulate throughout the settlement as if they owned it all in common. Bevies of little girls (and boys), some of them barely old enough to walk, push open the door of any kitchen, slide silently in, and arrange themselves on the daybed where they sit and giggle and observe.

During a single day, each of Elizabeth's seven children would bring three or more of their friends home at least once. Elizabeth seldom told any of the children to leave the house. If the family happened to be eating a meal, she often made room for them at the table to share the food. She always seemed to care and have time for everybody, hugging or giving a child a "ride" in the rocking chair. The same seemed to be the case with the other housewives in the neighbourhood, but the children seemed to have a couple of favourite kitchens, of which Elizabeth's was one.

Elizabeth, like most outport housewives, also entertains woman visitors in her kitchen daily and visits the kitchens of her closest neighbours regularly. Such visits may last a couple of hours but are more often of a short duration, sometimes only a few minutes. This is understandable considering her tight working schedule and the demands put on her by her children. Often, she has to steal away from her work: "I'm never able to finish anything. I just have to leave it"; or from her children: "I've fed them all now I think. I need a break before I start cleanin' up."

Sometimes the children would go looking for her. Coming up to our house they would ask "Is mom here? You know where she is?" For the children, mom and the house are one and an outport housewife rarely leaves the house for more than a few hours.

During their visits, the housewives chat. One needs no excuse to visit and nothing is offered the visitors except when the family itself is having a cup of tea or a meal. The housewife continues with her work while chatting although she usually "sits down for a minute."

The favourite topics of conversation are their working routines and breaks in the routine, the activities and personalities of their respective children, and not least, the state of their health. It should be noted that talk about poor health among the women does not generally have the same connotations as it does among many un- and under-employed men; that is, it is not part of a strategy of legitimizing disable-bodied pensions (cf. Ch. 4). The conversation may also revolve around bits of "news," such as a telephone call or a letter from kin in Toronto, a childbirth, wedding, or death in the community, a new purchase by one of the women or by someone in the village, and the like. Still, 'routine' topics dominate the conversation and the main function of the visits seems not to be to exchange new information; two or three women are capable of talking at the same time and about the same things over and over again.

The major functions of the visits thus are to provide a break from household chores and the opportunity for people to show concern for each other, especially for their kin and neighbours. Showing concern for kin and neighbours is an important outport value particularly among the married women; it is not limited to occasions when someone has experienced an accident. This continuous show of concern also seems to create strong bonds between women outside the kin groups.

The two determining factors of the composition of a housewife's visiting circle are neighbourhood and kinship. Often, of course, one's closest neighbours are one's kin. However, one's next-door neighbours will always belong to one's visiting circle regardless of whether they are kin or not or whether they are of the same generation. Close kin, sisters, daughters, sisters-in-law, and daughters-in-law who do not live too far away are generally also included.

Elizabeth's immediate visiting circle includes her husband's brother's wife, her husband's half-sister and her two brothers' wives. The two former are her next-door neighbours and the latter two live about a hundred yards down the road. It used to include her oldest daughter who lived next door but who left for Toronto. The circle also included her husband's first cousin's wife but since she "shifted," that is, moved a quarter of a mile up the road, they seldom see each other although, as both stated "we used to see each other every day before we shifted." There is another possible reason besides the break in contiguity for this drop in interaction: an increasing gap in social status between their husbands. This will be discussed in chapter 7.

Except for the changes referred to above, Elizabeth's daily interaction within the neighbourhood does not seem to have changed either in style or in personnel from what it used to be before her husband went on welfare. As shown earlier, her household routine does not seem to have changed much either. Elizabeth's network of interpersonal relations and her social standing, in contrast to her husband's, are much the same as they were.

The strain of "going on welfare" in a rural community thus seems to be greater for the husband than for the wife, in that the husband loses his main role in the family – that of provider. This situation has been described by several observers of the unemployed (for example, Bakke, 1940; Cavan and Ranck, 1938). Cavan, writing about unemployment in the United States in the 1930s, observed that "apparently actual reduction in dollars earned was less devastating than the change of roles; dire poverty was easier to bear than the husband's loss of status to some previously subordinate member (1959:404).

However, the role relationship between husband and wife is determined by more than the work they do. Although this in itself is important, roles

within the family are determined by less tangible factors which can be summarized under the heading of division of authority in contrast to the division
of labour. When George says he has a good wife, he is clearly praising her
for being not only a good worker, but also because she "behaves like a wife
should." As in most western rural societies, the Newfoundland wife is supposed to be subservient to her husband. If anything, this rule seems to be
stronger in the Newfoundland outports than in other areas of North America
and Europe (Faris, 1966:95–99). An outport wife is supposed to admit, at
least in public, that the husband is in charge – in the local language, that the
husband is "the skipper." Szwed, writing from a Newfoundland west coast
community, says that "Men are expected to be the judges of what is wise
for themselves and their families" (1966:83).

Elizabeth seems to find it natural to play the role of a good wife in this
sense. This is not surprising considering that she had been married to George
for twenty-seven years before he became unemployed. On the other hand,
it would have been easy and perhaps even 'natural' for Elizabeth to take
charge in the present situation, with George being "around the house" most
of the time. In fact, many other wives whose husbands are on able-bodied
relief or on a medical certificate seem to have done so.

For Elizabeth, supporting her husband in his role of authoritative head
of the household is clearly made easier because George is a good husband
in everything except for his not being able to earn a living. George "behaves";
his being on welfare has not involved him in any other negative forms of behaviour such as getting into undesirable company. This has happened to some
men who had to go on welfare (see Ch. 8). We can perhaps make the
generalization that the cultural rule which is that the husband is treated with
the respect due him as the head of the household is followed by the wife as
long as there are no good reasons *not* to do so.

Also, for a housewife such as Elizabeth who has less than good health, a
large family, and fewer amenities than her urban counterpart (running water,
oil heating, and others), it is clearly of great help to have her husband at
home and not leave the community to work for long periods. The best thing
would be, of course, for the husband to work locally. In some cases, a
housewife may prefer to have her husband staying home and not working at
all to working away; but for a husband to stay home if work is available
occurs only if the wife is incapable of taking care of her household and gets
a medical certificate (cf. Ch. 4).

If and when a wife "takes charge" of the family, it may involve a maternal
protective behaviour towards her husband, especially if he is on a medical
certificate. The wife of a man on able-bodied relief may also regularly tell
her husband what to do and contradict him or argue with him in the presence
of other people.

In our case, however, when Elizabeth and George were together in the presence of other people, she usually let George lead the conversation, and while George might sometimes interrupt his wife, she would seldom interrupt him. If she did, it would be in support of something he had said. Elizabeth supported her husband's statements when he was not present, also. I often overheard her state things that George had said some time before, almost verbatim, although not necessarily making any reference to him. Her support could also be seen in what she did *not* say. There were certainly many instances when she could have criticized George's activities as well as his statements but she never did so, at least not in public.

That is not to say that Elizabeth never initiated conversation herself. She constantly did so. But the topics did not in any way concern men, in general, and her husband, in particular. I wish to emphasize that Elizabeth in no way seemed to be dominated by her husband; within the confines of the outport wife role, she behaved freely and with great confidence.

In the preceding pages, I have qualified several statements with "at least not in public." This qualification is necessary on two accounts: first, because I never overheard a private conversation between husband and wife; and secondly, in public, it is most often the husband who gives the definitive word. There seems to be considerable sharing and cooperation between husband and wife in the actual decision-making process, according to several observers (Szwed, 1966; Faris, 1966; Chiaramonte, 1971) and many of my own informants, including George: "We always used to talk things over with the wife." The scene of much of this talking-over takes place in bed after the children have gone to sleep and after all visitors have gone. In a family with many children and with the layout of the outport house, this is about the only time a husband and wife have occasion to be alone.

Talking in bed is symbolic of another aspect of outport information management; namely, that husband and wife seldom or never talk about their basic problems or worries to other people. They seldom talk about financial problems or their marriage to close friends as is the custom among many urban middle-class westerners (see Paine, 1969).

This point is vividly brought out by Chiaramonte (1971) in a study of a South Coast outport community. Chiaramonte asked all his married informants whom they would talk to about their worries and they all answered, only to their spouse. When asked what they would do if their spouses were away and they had to make a decision, the reply was "wait 'till she (he) comes home." When pressed further and asked whom they would turn to if they were not in a position to wait (which was indeed implied in the first question), most of the informers said they would still wait, while some said he (she) would perhaps go to the postmaster. The postmaster, significantly, was from outside the community, and therefore, "a stranger."

In a dozen questionnaires which a research assistant conducted for me in Squid Cove, all but three male informants stated that they would not talk about their worries to anyone except their wives. One of the three, a man in his fifties, stated that he would talk to the welfare officer. Of the two other men, both in their twenties, one said he would talk to his father, and the other to a specified close friend. Of the housewives, only one stated that she would talk to a specific friend; the rest would talk only to their husbands.

It is probable that the exclusive sharing of problems by the husband and wife in outport culture, as well as the publicly subservient role the wives play, make it easier for a man on welfare not to show his dependence on his wife to the extent that he really is dependent. It is clear that a man on welfare relies greatly on his wife's *voluntary* support of his role as the head of the household, a role which came automatically when he was working and was the undisputed provider. Using an old cliché, one can say that the husband in George's situation has to be supported in his role more for what he is than for what he does.

It is significant that George never talked about this dependency directly. The furthest George went was to praise his wife in a general way: "I've had a good woman"; "I wouldn't have been able to do without her." Yet George and other men in the same situation seem to become more conscious of the importance of having a good wife in the broad sense discussed above.

The wife's duty to give voluntary role support to her husband is made possible by an internal accommodation between husband and wife; but there is still another problem: the spatial setting of role performances. If the wife is to maintain her social network with other women in the neighbourhood and hold their respect and friendship, and her husband his masculinity, he has to keep out of the women's territory. However, being on able-bodied relief implies that a man spends much of his time around the house, and this involves problems of "findin' something to do" which is not detrimental to his male role. If a man does not have too much to do, it would be convenient to spend much of his time in the house. However, in outport Newfoundland, the house is not the man's castle; it is the woman's. For a man, the house "is (only) where he eats his meals, sleeps, procreates and occasionally indulges in some special skill – carving a ship model, perhaps, or whittling out birch brooms" (Mowat, 1968).

Except for these occasions, the house is the territory of the housewife and a man will feel uneasy staying in it if he has nothing to do there. In an outport house, there is no 'men's room' where a man could carry on an activity. The main room of the house is the kitchen – the wife's workshop – where she also entertains her women visitors.

Even if a man had "nothing very much to do" preferring to sit in the kitchen for an hour or two after a meal, and this was acceptable to his wife, the woman-visiting would make him uneasy. On many occasions when Elizabeth had visitors and George was there, he would leave after a while remarking "I've some work to do." If my wife was among the visitors, he often came to our house where there were no women at the time and sat and talked to me for a couple of hours.

Husbands on medical certificates seem to stay in the house (or kitchen) more than men on able-bodied relief. There are at least two reasons for this: first, since they are "sick," it is more acceptable to themselves and to others "to stay inside"; and secondly, being sick, they are more likely to be sanctioned by the community if they are seen working too much (cf. Ch. 4).

If a man stays in the house, he has to accept the company of women if not necessarily interaction with them. Some try to keep the interaction to a minimum, but most gradually begin participating more and more in their chats, which, significantly, concentrate on matters of health. To other men in the community, such men are described as becoming "like women."

The 'man's house' in the outports is the so-called "store," a small building which, in fishing communities, is situated by the waterfront and, in logging communities, somewhere in the yard not far from the dwelling house. During the winter, when a fisherman is not fishing, and during the fishing season when the weather "ain't fit for fishing," he spends most of the day in his store (most household heads have one). Here men repair their gear and do other odd jobs; they also sit and chat with friends and fellow fishermen. Women seldom enter the store except when they are helping the men with the fish. Even when a fisherman has nothing to do, rather than stay in the house, he goes down to the store to take an after-meal nap.

The store in logging communities is not the institutionalized men's house it is in fishing communities. Not all loggers have a store where it is possible to stay on a cold day; some have only a wood shed. Significantly, George built a new "winter" store when he became unemployed and began lobster fishing; later, he put a stove in it so that he could work there. The store seems to play an important role in George's 'adaptation' to being unemployed. He spends much of his time there doing a number of odd jobs, especially when he has nothing else to do and the women occupy the house. Indeed, the store in itself, generates some work in the form of repairs and improvements. George's new working routines is the main theme of the following chapter.

"I've Enough to Do Around the House to Keep Me Busy"

The fact that George is unemployed for most of the year means that he has to spend much of his time "around the house." When he says "You don't know how hard it is for a man who's been workin' all his life suddenly not to have no work," he implies not only the loss of income and status from being unemployed but also the problem of finding something to do, not necessarily only employment. He often said "I have to have somethin' to keep me busy – a man has to have *somethin'* to do."

A typical day for George in the early fall was the following (approximate hours).

7 a.m.
got up, made the fire on the wood stove, fetched water, washed and shaved.
7:30
his wife got up; George had breakfast with the children, talked to wife and children; children prepared to go to school.
8:30
went out to haul his "herring net" set close to shore in the "cove," cleaned the boat and the fish, went over to one of his neighbours with some of the mackerel.
10:30
had a cup of tea in the house, talked to his wife, left the house shortly after a neighbour came to visit his wife.
11:00
brought up a load of pebbles from the beach to lay on the path in front of his house.
11:30
went to the shop up the road to buy some groceries, chatted with a number of men inside and outside the shop.
12:30 p.m.
had "dinner" with wife and children who came home from school.
1:30
cut a load of firewood, took some of it into the house and left some out to dry.
3:00
worked in "store," made a paddle for the speedboat.
5:00
supper with wife and children.
6:00
in the store again, patched a pair of rubber boots for one of his children, cleaned up the store.
7:00
cut the hair of one of his neighbours, conversed for some time before and after.
8:00
went to the neighbours' to watch a movie on television (George did not own a T.V. set at the time).

10:00
had "lunch," talked to wife and children and ethnographer; smaller children to bed.
11:30
went to bed after visitors left.

Altogether, these various activities added up to seven or eight hours, corresponding to an average work day. In comparison to other days, however,
it was a somewhat busy one for George. The average amount of time spent
"working" was between five and six hours over a period of three weeks, including a couple of days when he did not do much because of an "ache in
the back." As was indicated in chapter 4, the cause and effect is probably
the converse here; that is, the back ache may partly have been due to the
fact that he could find nothing worthwhile to do. When George states (as he
often did) that "I've enough work to do around the house to keep me busy,"
he is stating more what he wishes than what is really the case. While he might
find something to do to keep him busy most days, it is important that the task
have some meaning for him and it should be something which he feels has
to be done (keeping up the house, for example); also, it should involve
something that does not contradict his role as the head of the household, but
rather supports this role. The purpose of his work cannot be just to "have
somethin' to do." The regular daily activities are of particular importance
in that they supply him with the framework for a working routine. They include making a fire in the morning and supplying wood throughout the day,
fetching water from the well, and shopping. These tasks alone give him at
least three hours of work per day.

George may often delegate some of the daily tasks to his older children,
especially when he has something else to do. However, in doing so, he is
asserting his role as head of the household by giving an order: "John, you go
and get some wood – and do it now!"; or "Harry, you go and fetch some
water for your mother. You should help your mother."

George took over shopping from his wife when he became unemployed.
When he worked in the woods and stayed away from home for long periods,
his wife, of course, had to do much of it. Elizabeth, however, does not under-
mine the importance of who does the shopping at present. "I like to buy
things I see when I'm up there (in the shop) and we can't afford to, so it's
better stayin' home and not knowin' what is in there." Being in charge of
shopping gives George not only a daily task, but also makes it necessary for
his wife and other members of the household to ask him to buy this or that.
Even if the items which are bought have been decided on beforehand, the
procedure, one may even call it a ritual, acts to support his role as head of
the household.

The seemingly trivial task of making the fire every morning before the
rest of his household is up, George never delegates to anyone. By being the

first to get up and begin the daily chores, he exercises a kind of initiative over other members of the household; he begins the cycle. Again, most of the activities are generally set beforehand: his wife has to make breakfast and the cihldren have to go to school. However, there are always some activities which are not completely routinized and in which a decision must be taken; even in routine activities, the children have to be told to dress properly and to take care on the road, for example. George also tells his wife and children what he is going to do that day and how the family have to accommodate to his "doings." "I need your help with the nets this evenin' David, so don't be late from school"; or "I'm going to haul some firewood today and will be away most of the day so you be sure you fetch water for your mother, John."

George is not able to take much initiative in his wife's tasks by being first up in the morning. On the other hand, he need never be told by his wife to fetch water, for instance, or get firewood. He also gets his wife's gratitude for being able to come into a warm kitchen every morning; George is very proud in pointing out that in the last several years, he has over-slept only once.

In this connection, we should note that it is the lack of amenities which forms the basis of much of George's routine work. The installation of an oil stove in the kitchen instead of the present wood stove would mean one less daily task. Many of his neighbours, especially the younger men not locally employed, but also others, have installed combined wood/oil stoves. The basic reason why George has not done so is certainly because of the cost involved, but he also constantly pointed out that he "likes the wood stove better."

Similarly, the installation of plumbing in the kitchen would not involve great costs if one made use of natural gravity. Most of George's neighbours have rigged up a running water system in this way. Elizabeth remarked several times that "water in the house" would be very convenient for her. George, however, concentrates on the negative sides of it: that the water is more likely to freeze, that it might not taste as good because they would have to dig another well to make use of the gravity, and that a well "up the hill" might easily dry up. George is right in all these statements. In dry summers, for instance, many neighbours have had to get water from George's well since it is the last to dry up. Yet, the fact that he overcommunicates the drawbacks of installing a pump and oil-stove and undercommunicates the positive sides, seems to indicate that he is also aware that the installation of these facilities would reduce his work role.

In addition to the regular daily tasks described above, George spends a large proportion of his time making various repairs and improvements on his house and property. During the fall of 1968, he painted the house, tarred the roof, repaired leaks in the roof and one of the windows, and set up a new fence. Inside the house, he put new "canvas" on the kitchen floor, boarded the walls with "Canada boards," and painted various things. Most of these jobs lasted for several days, from five to eight hours a day.

George's concern for his house is in keeping with a general outport value which has been remarked upon by several observers. Iverson and Matthews (1968:122), in their study of resettlement in outport communities, report "The importance the rural Newfoundlanders attach to their house is reflected in the care they give it. With striking regularity we found that the houses of natives and newcomers alike were well cared for, despite the meager resources." I did not get the impression that George did more work on his house than was normal in the community, although he might have spent more time at it. This may be because of the lack of money, as he complained several times that he did not have enough money to buy new material but had to make do with "old stuff." Also, it is probable that the various repairs which George made on his house had an additional value for him compared to employed men, and, indeed, to George himself before he became unemployed; they gave him something meaningful to do.

While the daily tasks referred to earlier could be performed by any of his older boys since they did not demand special skills, the repair work George did on his house required skill that only he possessed in the household. The older boys might help him occasionally, but they were never allowed to take it over and George constantly informed them of their inability to do that kind of work; their inability was largely due to his not teaching them the necessary skills, so that he could tell them how it should be done and order them around.

For an unemployed man, then, not only employment but also "work around the house" becomes a limited good. In this respect, the rural unemployed man who owns his house has an advantage over the urban unemployed. The house provides him with something to do – work that is directly relevant to the rest of the household and acts to maintain his role of head of household.

So far I have indicated that work around the house is the only type of work open to men such as George. That is of course not the case; unemployed men in the outports can also exploit the various local resources. The Squid Cove area allows for a variety of subsistence activities. Most of them are seasonal, however, and give rise to a rather complex ecological year (see Table 3, below).

Except for lobster, none of these resources are exploited commercially by George or most men on able-bodied relief in Squid Cove. Some may "try to earn a dollar" by selling various game, fish, or firewood. However, the amount of cash earned this way is minimal. There are at least three reasons for this: (1) the resources are limited; (2) many people (including those who hold regular jobs) are "at it"; and (3) an excessive amount of subsis-

TABLE 3

Annual Seasonal Cycle

Activity \ Time	Jan	Feb	Mar	Apr	May	June	July	Aug	Sept	Oct	Nov	Dec
Firewood												
getting in	—	—										
cutting				—	—					—	—	
Bird hunting	—											
Sealing		—	—									
Lobster fishing												
preparing for		—	—									
catching				—	—	—						
Fishing					—	—	—	—	—	—		
Rabbit snaring										—	—	
Moosehunting										—	—	
Gardening					—	—	—	—	—	—		

tence products such as fish and game not immediately consumed by one's own household are, according to local custom, supposed to be given away to kin and neighbours as gifts. Also, with regard to firewood, many of the potential customers, that is men with full-time jobs, have installed oil heating.

The economic returns from these various activities are, then, rather small and one may wonder why men engage in them at all. It could be argued that for the men on able-bodied relief, their opportunity costs are zero since they are not employed; on the other hand, pursuing most of the subsistence activities involves cash outlays which are scarce.

Whereas the commercial value of the local resources is modest, the subsistence value can be relatively great. For George and his family, it adds up to more than 10 percent of the total real income (cf. Table 2 in ch. 2), fish and firewood making up the main subsistence items; for other households, agricultural and animal products rank the highest. The types of subsistence production that will be of greatest importance in an area are, of course, largely dependent on the resource base. In the present context, however, we are especially interested in differences in the involvement in subsistence production between the employed and the unemployed; as one might expect, the unemployed come out on top. In the language of the economists, the opportunity costs for the unemployed are zero since they have no alternative uses for their time. On the other hand, the difference in involvement between the two categories is not as great as one might have thought and two factors might explain this. First, most men in Squid Cove are employed only seasonally and, second, pursuing most of the subsistence activities often involves considerable cash outlays, in which respect the unemployed are at a disadvantage.

Pursuing subsistence activities also has significant social, as distinct from economic, constraints. Most of these activities require a partner or "buddy." This is so because some activities, especially those at sea, require at least two persons: one to navigate the boat and one to perform the actual fishing or hunting. Then, there is the element of risk involved in fishing or hunting on one's own often far from any settlement. There are many local stories about people who got lost or who only just managed to make it back to the community. A buddy may also be needed for adding complementary equipment and/or skills to the activity; one man may have the speedboat and outboard engine while the other the right kind of gun and be a "good shot." Finally, a buddy provides company and an audience for exhibiting one's skill and manliness. This purely social factor is not least in importance.

In most of the subsistence activities which George engaged in since he became unemployed – fishing, sealing, and hunting – he used one (or two) of his sons as his buddy. Having grown-up sons able to fulfill this role was, no doubt, important to George, and he would not have been able to pursue some of the activities without them. This became obvious when his two oldest sons went to Toronto to work. During that time, George did not go bird hunting ("birding") or sealing at all and went fishing less often than he did when they were at home. To some extent, the ethnographer acted as a substitute and indeed, George's wife compared my role to that of the oldest son. His school-aged sons, although "big enough" to be his buddies, were generally able to help him only during the summer months and the weekends.

However, even if George had had a grown-up son to "buddy up with" all the time, he would still not have fulfilled the same role as a "real" buddy. For one thing, his oldest sons often went fishing and hunting with their peers rather than with their father. Eric remarked that his father restrained the activities by "not bein' willin' to take any chances," and George would say that Eric was "too hard for him to follow" and that he "took too many chances." Eric thus often joined a next-door neighbour of his own age, and a son of William's who was George's number-one buddy (see below).

Another reason why his sons could not become real buddies to George was the mere fact that they were his sons. Although his own sons, especially Eric, could be as good buddies as anyone else George worked with, instrumentally, they were not able to provide some of the social aspects which another person could. Had his sons been married, with their primary loyalties to their own nuclear families, the situation might have been different. In fact, many men on welfare do have married sons as their closest buddies. The difference between a married son, and an unmarried and younger son, seems to lie in the greater voluntary nature of the establishment of a buddy relationship with the former: with younger unmarried sons, the wish of the "old man" to buddy up with them would likely be taken as a command, while older married sons would be thought to have minds of their own.

A natural buddy for George would have been his youngest brother, Carl, who lived next door and who was also unemployed for a large part of 1968. However, although George and Carl saw each other almost every day and they were on friendly terms, they only occasionally engaged in subsistence activities together. The main reason for this seems to have been his brother's demographic situation. Carl had three sons who were all married and two of whom built their houses next door to their father. All his sons worked away and Carl spent a lot of time helping them with their houses when they were home and helping his daughters-in-law with various things when they were not. Carl also succeeded in getting more casual employment than George, being a relatively skilled carpenter. Thus, his work and his proximity to his sons occupied Carl to the extent that he had little time for subsistence activities, except in the winter time when he cut and hauled firewood.

George's other brother Stanley who also lives close by was not available either. Because of his heart condition, he qualified for a medical certificate, and earned extra money by selling firewood locally. The fact that he did this and owned an old truck, as well, caused people to resent him because he was on a medical certificate. For these reasons, Stanley had more or less withdrawn from the community, and during my stay, I saw him visiting George only half a dozen times. Several years ago, before Stanley acquired a medical certificate, George and Stanley had been fishing buddies and still owned some nets together.

Most of George's other neighbours work in the woods or have other non-local jobs and are home only on the weekends. The only time a number of local men are available is during the winter months when, with the exception of getting firewood, few subsistence activities are engaged in. Yet, for George to have buddied up with another unemployed man on welfare would have been sanctioned negatively by his employed friends. This point will be analysed in greater detail in the following chapters. Thus, within his own neighbourhood, George did not have many potential buddies besides his own sons. He could have gone outside the neighbourhood to find someone but that would have been inconvenient, especially without a car.

It was, therefore, a great comfort to George when a close neighbour, William, aged sixty, returned from Toronto early in the fall and stayed home through the winter. William and George became buddies soon afterwards: they went rabbit-snaring together, fishing and wood-cutting, and later moose-hunting. William also served as a companion. The fact that William's own sons except one (Eric's buddy), were working in Toronto, and that William had no other relatives in the community (an unusual situation in Squid Cove) also made George more important to William.

Besides creating "something to do" and dyadic relationships, subsistence activities are important to both the unemployed and the employed in that they constitute a sport or relaxing pastime. But more than this, for many outporters – employed or not – hunting and fishing are "the real things in life," and much of their income is spent on equipment necessary to pursue such activities: a speedboat, outboard engine, fishing gear, shotguns, rifles, and even a car may be bought for this purpose.

To the extent that the unemployed can afford to engage in these sport/ subsistence activities, they share a common sub-culture with the employed which may compensate, to some extent, for the fact that they do not share the sub-culture of work. For George, the moose-hunt he took part in during the 1968 season greatly undermined the fact that he was on able-bodied relief. George had not been moose-hunting for several years, the major reason being that the moose population which was accessible on foot had been declining drastically because of the building of roads through the area. To go moose-hunting with some hope of "a kill," one had to travel thirty to one hundred miles away and this necessitated a car. Neither George nor his potential partners had a car. The 1968 hunt was made possible because the ethnographer had a car and was eager to go moose-hunting, partly because this was a new experience for him, and partly because George had talked a lot about previous hunts and his desire to go again.

Moose-hunting, compared to other types of hunting, may have considerable economic returns. The license fee is only fifteen dollars (ten for former license holders) and the result might be four hundred pounds of meat. George and his wife often remarked throughout the fall how nice it would have been to have had "that much 'fresh,' especially for a big crowd like ours." The children, especially the boys, were also excited over the prospect of their father getting a moose, and the hunt was the main topic of conversation among everyone in the neighbourhood for the time it lasted (November through December).

Our hunt began with short daily trips not too far away, but as we did not find anything, we took longer trips and stayed overnight in various log cabins a few miles from the road. However, we did not succeed in killing a moose until we got help from an old "friend" of George's who "was a good shot." Although it was disappointing for George not to have killed the moose himself, at least he "got his moose" and more than four hundred pounds of meat to share.

There can be no doubt that the moose meant a lot to George. It not only gave him "something to do," but also involved him in much social interaction during the actual hunt. After the hunt, there was more work in cleaning, butchering, and hanging up the carcass in George's store; and later, trips to the store to "cut a slice for dinner," or for a "snack in the evening." Also, the hunt was a topic of conversation for the people who came to view the moose. Thus, both the actual hunt and the residual activities increased the range of George's social interaction for some time.

The building and repairing of boats and houses and even the collection of firewood also have a sport-like and hence, social aspect in the outports. For instance, in selecting the area where one is going to cut firewood or building material, it is important to pick an area with good wood. "Good" in this context means several things: that the wood-stand one is cutting from is dense, that the wood is large, and that it is easy to haul out. Men collect social rewards from other men on the basis of such criteria. When the wood is piled up close to the road, the amount and kind of wood a man has collected is viewed and assessed by other men in the community. "George has a nice bit of wood there" or similar remarks are heard constantly.

It is quite apparent how 'woods' activities provide a subject for conversation among the men who rely on it for firewood and building purposes. Men with a more traditional adaptation are always on the look-out for potential wood-stands whenever they travel in the woods on hunting or fishing trips. Some men would remember for years single trees they had come across and which could be used for a specific purpose such as boat-building. Most men have considerable knowledge about the wood in the immediate surrounding area, not necessarily because they have been there, but as much because they have accumulated information in numerous informal conversations. A man with special knowledge of the local territory is endowed with a lot of social prestige and a man on welfare often has more information than a man who has been working all the time.

Commentaries on other men's work, especially on the building of houses and boats, is a popular topic of conversation. They may be positive or negative, but negative criticism is seldom made in face-to-face interactions with the craftsmen but rather between two or more men commenting on the work of a man not present. Negative comments serve as a sign of the commentator's own skill and add to his self-confidence. The remarks are often detailed and a man may elaborate on how *he* would have done the work; or they may be very short: "That's not very good work; he could have taken more time and done a better job." Positive face-to-face comments serve to give the craftsman self-respect and prestige or, if nothing else, they show interest. As one man said, comparing the outport he used to live in with the urban area he presently lives in, "In a small community, you are being noticed for what you are doing. Each one helps to build up the other – makes each one feel important. In a town it's only your family."

The above observation highlights the turn of the argument in this chapter; namely, from the importance of subsistence activities (in the sense of doing-things-for-oneself) as providers of 'something to do" and augmenters of 'real' income to their part played in maintaining social relations. The many possibilities in the outports (and presumably in rural areas in general) of engaging in various productive activities, even when unemployed, make it easier for a man to maintain his role as head of household compared to his counterpart in the city (cf. Liebow, 1967; Hannerz, 1969). Furthermore, we can distinguish some subsistence activities as having their main function in maintaining the head-of-household role *within the family* and others which are more important in maintaining this role *outside the family* – in relation to other men. In contrast to what seems to be the case among many urban unemployed (*op. cit.*), there are no contradictions in the outports between the assertion of the head-of-household role within and outside the family.

George often told me that he had lots of friends in Squid Cove as well as in other neighbouring communities. His use of the term friend, however, would often be all-embracing: "We are all friends, you might say, around here" referring to the fact that in Squid Cove and surrounding area, "everybody knew everybody else." He also seemed to include among his friends anyone who was not an enemy: "I've no enemies around here as far as I know – no one would have any reason to be anyhow."

Generally, when George used the term friends he used two criteria: he included everybody he had known over a period of time *and* who behaved towards him "like they always used to"; that is, did not treat him differently since he became unemployed. He, therefore, considered the community merchant his friend. "I traded with the Brown's for more than thirty years, and I can go to John any time (to buy on credit). He's never said no to me: John's a good friend of mine."

George's relationship with the merchant is clearly not symmetrical in the sense that the merchant would call George a friend, nor in the sense that the same type of prestations are exchanged. According to Pitt-Rivers (1963) and Wolf (1966), this is a "lop-sided" friendship or a patron-client relationship. It is similar to many notions of friendship in that it is personal, private, and informal, but different from a friendship relationship in that it is asymmetrical (see Paine, 1969).

George also included among his 'friends' a number of men from Squid Cove and other communities with whom he once worked. They were some of the partners George had in his long career as a logger, and out of these relationships there sometimes emerged interaction of a more social than task-specific nature. George still talks about these former workmates as his friends although he may not have seen them for several years. "There's a fellow down there in Fearless Cove. We used to be buddies in the woods. He was always a good friend. He's been the same all the time. He'll always come down to the house when he's around here. It's been a while since I saw him, all the same."

During my six months as George's next-door neighbour, I did not see him visited by more than two of his former workmates from outside his own community. However, these two visits were "friendly" and pleased George very much. He talked about them several times afterwards to me and to his other neighbours, emphasizing how "good a friend" and how "nice a fellow" the visitor was. Thus, it was of great importance to George that he could regard former workmates as being his friends, particularly in relation to his neighbours. When he was working, George could make his neighbours believe that he had a number of friends among his workmates, whether they visited him or not. In his present situation, however, the visiting has become the diacritica of their existence, and his neighbours could easily see if he had visitors or not. Since he became unemployed, George's relationships outside the community have, in a sense, become more public.

Partly because George seldom sees these "friends," and partly because these relationships do not seem to be very intimate and private, I would be inclined to call them "less than friendships" – that is, acquaintanceships (see Paine, 1969). It should be noted that the "buddy" relationship discussed in the preceding chapter also shows significant differences from a friendship, at least as it is conceptualized in the Western urban middle-class culture. First of all, it is task-oriented and its establishment is related to the ecological and economic circumstances in the outport communities. Buddies need not and often do not interact in any other capacity than the one they have "buddied up for"; a moose hunt, for example.

Thus, buddies need not have much more in common than an interest in the specific activity in question. This can be seen in the fact that buddies often belong to different socio-economic groups; for example, in Squid Cove, a merchant could go moose-hunting with an ordinary fisherman who happens to be a "good shot"; the school principal, the doctor, and the welfare officer may do the same. Such buddy relationships play an important part in boosting the self-esteem of the partner of the lower social standing, and they also give an image of the community that is more egalitarian than it really is. George told me about one moose hunt several times when he "buddied up with" one of the local merchants. "We shared everything. There was no difference between us then. I was as good as him."

The buddy relationship thus shares with the friendship relationship its egalitarian nature, but the egalitarianism is limited to the activity in question. The relationship of confidence is consequently highly qualified in contrast to that between close friends in a middle-class culture (Paine, 1969). Nevertheless, even within the actual activity, the confidence may be a long-term one. A buddy partnership may be restricted to a single moose hunt; the next season, one may have another buddy and yet there would not normally be any ill feeling between the men because of this as long as they were both able to secure new buddies. "Me and Pete have been buddies for the last two years, but this year Pete is goin' with another fellow. I'm takin' my brother as my buddy this year."

Relations between neighbours (and also kin, see below) distinguish themselves from buddy relations and from acquaintanceships in that they are (generally) more permanent and involve frequent interaction in many capacities. Relations between neighbours are also symmetrical in that they use reciprocal terms and exchange more or less the same types of prestations.

George talked highly about his neighbours, calling them friends, and his neighbours reciprocated and said that George was "a good neighbour." I heard only a few of the neighbours use the term friend when talking about George. On the other hand, everyone talked to me about the neighbourliness which existed in the neighbourhood. George would comment:

There's nowhere around here (in the neighbourhood) that you won't get anything if you need something – small things, that is.

I never said no to no one coming to borrow something that I've got, like a saw or a scythe or something. If I'm not home, they'll ask Elizabeth and she'll tell them to go and take it (from the store). You may want something yourself anytime.

The only thing I'm a little particular about is my saw. If someone borrows my saw and brings her back in bad shape, I don't like that.

The type of neighbourly help which George most often extends, besides lending his various tools, consists of aiding his neighbours having difficulties carrying out some activities on their own, such as launching a boat, repairing or putting up a house; and secondly, sharing the various kinds of subsistence products. George seemed to be more generous than most of his neighbours. "We (including his sons) sell nothin' of what we gets (from the sea) – we give it away for people to have a feed. We didn't sell any seal meat last spring except for a few pounds. We didn't have no more than three meals ourselves out of the two seals we got – almost everyone around here got a meal."

He seemed to be somewhat resentful about his neighbour's selling meat while not feeling free to do so himself. "Some people sell even to their neighbours, all the same. It costs something to get fish, seals and birds – shot and gas – so one should be able to sell something. Some people got thirty or forty cents a pound when they sold seal meat."

If George could not see *himself* selling fish, seal, or birds to his neighbours when he had a good catch, he would sometimes allow his sons to do it "to get some pocket money for themselves." Once when he had caught several dozens of mackerel, he allowed his sons, David and John (who had helped haul the net), to sell some of it in the neighbourhood. The boys came back to their father very enthusiastic and told him that they had sold twenty mackerel for fifteen cents a piece, and said: "We could have sold forty more. Why don't we sell all?" George got rather angry about this suggestion and replied, "Now look, who's the boss? You shouldn't say a thing like that. We can't sell all."

There is no doubt that George and the boys could have used the cash earned from selling some of their subsistence products and throughout the year, it might have added a couple of hundred dollars to the household income. However, the value of neighbourliness seems to be of greater importance to George, than what he might add to his household budget.

Although it appears that George is more concerned about sharing than most of his neighbours, and one might infer that this is in keeping with his (present) greater concern with acceptance in the community, his neighbours do not seem to feel that his generosity has increased since he became unemployed. Neighbours remarked that George "has always been like that," and George himself says that "it's something we always does." On the other hand, it is clear that George, with the help of his grown-up boys, produces more subsistence goods than he used to because he is home most of the year.

George's neighbours sometimes reciprocate without much delay. On other occasions, there may be a lapse of several months before a prestation is repaid, but the counter-prestation may be implicitly agreed upon beforehand. For example, one of George's neighbours has a horse which he uses primarily for hauling firewood; but he had very little pasture for growing hay for winter feed. George owned some pasture land and allowed his neighbour to cut the grass in return for the use of the horse for hauling his own firewood.

Both types of exchange show a "balanced reciprocity" (Sahlins, 1965: 147–48), although it sometimes seemed of great importance that the repayment not be immediate. Yet, if someone (as I, in my ignorance, did a few times) tried to repay a service immediately – one which is given "between neighbours" – the giver would feel extremely embarrassed; the custom is to wait at least a day or so. Most neighbourly help, however, seems to be given without any definite expectation of a return; it is "general reciprocity" in Sahlins' scheme (*ibid*). That is not to say that such prestations generate no counter-obligations, but they (the counter-obligations) are diffuse and determined by the need of the donor and/or possibility for the recipient to reciprocate. When such free gifts are made to a neighbour, the donor feels less hesitant about asking that neighbour for a "helping hand" or for a few tools. Indeed, a man might give his neighbour a gift in the anticipation that he will need that neighbour's help in the near future, but without stating so explicitly.

This right to give gifts, and the neighbours' obligation to accept (Mauss, 1954), play an important role in maintaining flexibility in the exchanges between neighbours. This aspect of neighbourliness has been important to George since he became unemployed. In his present situation, being unemployed and, indeed, having problems in finding something to do, George is in less need than his working neighbours for a helping hand or for subsistence products. Also, he has as large a collection of tools as his neighbours do. What George wants in return seems not primarily counter-prestations of the same kind, but rather acceptance and assurance that everything is as before. The fact that there is no rule of *exact* balanced reciprocity between neighbours and that one is allowed to insist on not wanting anything (material) in return, makes it possible for George to give 'material' services and receive 'social' services such as signs of acceptance. In other words, the outport institution of neighbourliness gives George and other unemployed men an opportunity to take initiative and to convert a property of the unemployment situation, namely time, into social assets: acceptance and assurance.

The type of relationship we are dealing with here is more accurately called neighbourliness than friendship. In a Newfoundland outport community (or neighbourhood within a larger community), neighbourliness is mandatory in the sense that a man (or woman) can ask a neighbour for various kinds of help and the latter cannot refuse to give it. Neighbour-relations are different from friendship relations in that one does not choose one's neighbours. They are also different in that a great deal of information is trafficked and in that they have a clear "surface" character (Paine, 1969:515). Like friends (and unlike most acquaintances), however, neighbours normally possess much information about each other and thus evaluate each other as total social persons.

Besides the merchant, former workmates, buddies, and neighbours, George includes most of his close kin (including affines) among his friends. There is a good deal of overlap here in that a number of his closest kin are also his neighbours and former buddies. Close kin residing in his neighbourhood include his younger brothers Stanley and Carl, four married brother's sons (three of Carl's and one of Stanley's), and a half-sister and her husband. George also has two of his wife's brothers as neighbours. In this respect, his situation is somewhat exceptional in that most other neighbours, including his two brothers, are married to non-local women and have none of their wives' kin living in the neighbourhood. This gives George the most extensive kin network in the neighbourhood. He also has three first cousins (father's brother's sons) as neighbours. As mentioned earlier, one of George's daughters also used to live next-door with her family before they moved to Toronto.

George has a number of kin in neighbouring communities, also. Two of his daughters are married and live ten and six miles away. (One of his daughters and her husband came back from Toronto the year after I left.) Another half-sister is married to a fisherman in still another community seven miles away, and his wife has a sister married to a logger five miles away.

All the kin mentioned above George regards as "close" and talks about as friends. This network is illustrated in the way George shared his moose (see Table 4, below).

TABLE 4

George's Distribution of His Moose

Own children's households	3
Own brothers' and sister's households	4
Wife's brothers' and sister's households	3
Nephews' (brother's sons) households	3
First cousins' households	2
Non-related households (helped with hunt)	2
Total number of households shared moose with	17

It should be noted that George's four next-door non-kin neighbours had been moose hunting themselves; otherwise, they would have been included.

George's relationship to some, if not all his relatives comes closest to the Western urban middle-class concept of friendship. Indeed, when I asked George whom he regarded as his closest friends, he first mentioned his two brothers and his wife's two brothers and then his next-door neighbour William (see Ch. 6). He talked about his other relatives as "good friends," but did not include them among his closest friends. Significantly, all the relatives George considered his closest friends were also close neighbours.

Where the interaction with relatives is perhaps most similar to interaction between friends in a middle-class culture is in what we may call sociability and privacy. For instance, the close relatives are the only households whom George and Elizabeth would visit together as a couple, and who would visit George and his wife as a couple. The kind of conversations they engage in are also of a more private nature than that between non-related neighbours and, in George's case, his buddies: family matters which they would expect the relatives to be interested in and to understand. It should be emphasized (as noted in Ch. 5) that intimate talk occurs only between husband and wife (cf. Chiaramonte, 1971).

A significant factor about George's (and Elizabeth's) close relatives is that none of them is on welfare. One could, perhaps, expect that being the only one in the family on welfare would have put George in an awkward situation. If this were the case, it did not show in their behaviour towards George. On the contrary, they all seem to accept that his being on welfare "is not his own fault," that he is not to blame. Yet, on several occasions when I was discussing people on welfare with some of these relatives, they spoke negatively about welfare recipients in general, but then, treated George as an exception without changing their general attitude.

George, on his part, always talks highly about his close relatives to other people and stresses the fact that they were "good workers" and that some "earned a lot of money." He seems to interact more with his kin/neighbours than he used to do before he became unemployed. One obvious reason for this is that he has more time than he used to. Another reason, just as important, is the fact that relationships to kin and neighbours are ascriptive and not directly related to the work role or other achieved roles. George might be said to have a right to be accepted by neighbours and especially by kin whether he is employed or not. At the same time, his kin can justify their interaction with him to their friends on the grounds that they cannot refuse to interact with a close relative. In other words, they feel obligated to him.

At the same time, George seemed to want to be able to talk more intimately about his problems, to explain more fully his situation and have his relatives accept his social worth not just on the grounds that he was a relative, but because he was a man. Although he never said so, I had a feeling that he suspected some of his close relatives and neighbours of talking positively about him as much to protect their own image as out of genuine respect for George.

The only "real" friend George seems to have among his kin is one of his brothers-in-law, Christopher. As far as I could establish, George's close relationship to him was of recent origin, having developed in the last few years when George was having difficulty in finding employment and had to go on welfare.

Christopher is in his late thirties and thus many years younger than George. He is married and has several children, the oldest being in his early teens. He is also a woodsman, driving heavy equipment for the same company as George used to work for. He is home only on week-ends and during the slack periods in the winter. George's interaction with Chris is thus limited but he visits him almost every week-end in his house. Chris also visits George but much less often than George visits him.

George talks more warmly about Christopher than about any of his other "friends." "He's a good man. He'll do anything for you. You wouldn't know he was a sinner"; or "You don't find a better person around here. He don't know the best to do for you."

George often takes various subsistence products over to Chris' sometimes even before Chris comes home for the week-end: "I was down to Chris' with some britches (fish roe). He likes that, you know. He'll get himself a good meal, when he gets home." When George was distributing his moose, he was very particular "to get a good piece for Chris." Chris, in turn, would overcommunicate the value of the gifts he received from George, but I never heard Chris talk as highly about George as George did about Chris. However, even in Chris' ordinary greeting – "How are you boy?" – I had an impression of a feeling of warmth for George. He also recognized George's worth and was sympathetic in his interaction with George. For instance, he often said, "You've done your lot, George. You've worked hard." George himself liked to repeat this statement to other neighbours and to me. More than anything else, it was what he wanted to hear said about himself.

What Chris gave George was a *sense of worth*; he seemed to understand his situation the way George felt it ought to be understood. The relationship was definitely more important to George than to Chris and, in that sense, not a symmetrical relationship but rather a lop-sided friendship. George seemed to be aware of the asymmetry in their relationship. However, in contrast to George's reaction to the asymmetry in other relations, it did not seem to matter with Chris. One reason for this is presumably the fact that Chris had no one else in the neighbourhood, except his brother, whom he felt closer to than George. This priority was important to George. Although he never put it this way, he seemed to be saying that "Chris's best friend around here (except for his own brother) is me!" When George states that Chris will do anything for you, "you" is not anybody, but George.

It is also significant that the kind of closeness and acceptance George gets from Chris, he also gets to a large extent from his own brother and next-door neighbour, Carl. However, to be favoured by a person who is not motivated by duty is a greater indication of acceptance.

It is clear that George succeeded in maintaining social relations as an *unemployed* person with some of his friends, neighbours, and kin who were *employed*. By interacting with George and approving of him, they supported and, in fact, *carried* his status in the moral community (see Ch. 10 for discussion of Squid Cove moral community). However, he did have difficulty in preventing some relationships from degenerating; hence they became asymmetrical. Interaction with friends involves more than exchanges of goods and services, talk and visits; much of it involves the exchange of information, advice, and support. George had more subsistence goods and more time to give away than most of his friends, but he had considerably less to offer of the other goods. Since he was not working and thus did not "get around very much," his stock of information tended to be small and most important, it was not renewed. The kind of information he had the most of was related to local affairs and local resources.

George tried to pick up other bits of information in various ways. His daily shopping trips gave him an opportunity to gather news. The shop is perhaps the most important place for exchanging information in outport communities (cf. Faris, 1966). George's children, who got around in the community much more than George did, were also a valuable source. Children are regarded as non-persons and, therefore, are allowed to be present where George would have to have had a reason to be present (cf. Faris, 1966; Chiaramonte, 1971). However, information acquired from the children, especially the smaller ones, is not always reliable and could not be used in adult conversations.

Other sources of information open to George were the radio and the television. George listened to the weather forecasts and the news several times a day. Even if others did the same, and the information was thus "not news," it could be used to initiate conversations and to further comments. "I heard on the news today that the government is goin' to pave the road down here. Now, when do you think that will happen?" Being illiterate, George was excluded from written sources: the occasional newspaper that reaches his house, the shopping catalogues, and the bulletins pinned up in the shops (of purchases and sales, meetings, and so on).

George's ability to give advice depended to a great extent on his having acquired information on new methods and materials for building, for example. In other words, his knowledge was restricted to subsistence production: how to file a saw, where to put a net to catch fish, or how to build a lobster pot.

In this connection, it should be noted that the type of advice given to neighbours in a Newfoundland outport is not of the private and intimate kind which is common among friends in our Western urban middle-class culture. As Matthews notes (Iverson and Matthews, 1968:25–26), "it is much easier to give advice to people in the city than in the country. For, in the city, the person who gives poor advice to a friend can avoid him and save himself embarrassment. In a rural community, this is almost impossible since people can hardly escape day-to-day contact. Thus, one hesitates to give advice in a small community."

Having information is especially relevant in supporting the statements of a neighbour or friend in a three-man conversation. An actual encounter may illustrate this. George and his next-door neighbour William were talking with a man from a neighbouring community. William was leading the conversation and was giving the other man his opinion on a political matter. The man was skeptical and George did not say anything for or against. William then asked, "Well, isn't that so George?" George, having little information about the matter, replied: "I wouldn't know about that, but I know some time ago ..." and he began to tell a story that was rather irrelevant to the topic. William interrupted him after a short while before he had finished his story, and argued his case without asking for George's support any more.

The support which George is able to give his friends seems to be of less value because he is not working. In sum, the type of information, advice, and support which George can give is restricted to local things or to non-local topics based on his *past* experience. George thus tells the same stories, gives the same information, and the same kind of advice over and over again. This has the effect of making him somewhat of a bore in many conversations. In this respect, George has entered the "old person" role prematurely. Like old people, he has a tendency to talk too much about the past and to be irrelevant; people may listen but pay little attention and make few comments and the conversation often takes the form of monologues. In other words, George imposes himself on his friends.

At the same time, George seems to need to participate in such chats more now than when he was working. In the absence of formal situations, notably the work situation, he has to use informal occasions to validate himself. Not to talk in these informal encounters would be as bad as talking too much.

George is also concerned that he reciprocates in his relations with his kin, neighbours, and buddies. To accept information, advice, and support, as well as goods and services, without being able to give something of equal value in return, although not necessarily the same thing, makes him feel bad, and not up to par as a friend.

A basic prerequisite for feeling equal, then, is that one has certain critical attributes in common with others and one of these attributes seems to be work. It is difficult to isolate the relative value of the work status itself: that one is earning one's living; and of the implications of the work status: that through work, one acquires assets which can be converted into information, advice, and support. What is clear is that both these components are relevant, and that both make it difficult to maintain relations of equivalence between unemployed and employed men; even though kinship and neighbour statuses are, or seem to be, independent of the work status, these statuses are not always easy to separate in actual encounters. Both kin and neighbours talk about their respective jobs *as* kin and neighbours, and the kin and neighbours without work are seriously disadvantaged.

In such a situation, one would find it natural for unemployed men to seek the company of men with more equal attributes, that is, other unemployed men. This is, in fact, how George and other men in his situation are going about their problem. However, this change in interaction often makes difficult simultaneous interaction with employed friends. When a person begins to choose 'interaction partners' from other categories than those specified by the informal rules, that is, from kin, neighbours, and friends (which overlap), then his behaviour will likely cause controversy in the moral community. Such difficulties will be the main theme of the following chapter.

8

Since George became unemployed and had to go on welfare, he has increased his interaction with other welfare recipients in Squid Cove. This increase is derived from two factors which should be distinguished: interaction which happened by chance and interaction which is intentionally sought by George himself.

The first type of interaction tends to occur simply because the number of welfare recipients in Squid Cove has increased drastically in the last few years (cf. Ch. 1). Then, since the welfare recipients are present in the community most of the time, the chances of George running into them are greater than if he had been employed. In fact, the geography of Squid Cove makes for increasing interaction in George's case. The main road passes close to George's house and anybody who walks on the road would have George within talking distance if he should happen to be outside his house. Also, people from the other neighbourhoods in the community have to pass George's house to get to the main stores, the doctor, the school, as well as to the closest neighbouring community. For George to refuse to exchange at least a few remarks would be against the moral order of the community, whoever the person may be (cf. Faris, 1966).

The other welfare recipients in the community found it easier to begin a conversation with George after he (also) went on welfare. Previously they might have greeted him shortly when they met him; now they stop and have a chat, and George always responds. However, with some recipients who have been on welfare for a long time and therefore might have a low social standing in the community, he often cuts the conversation short by saying, for example: "Now, I guess I have to go and do some work." On the other hand, George may also use such casual encounters to seek further interaction. An actual incident is worthwhile reporting since it also provides clues as to why such interaction is sought.

One early afternoon, George was standing outside his house having a smoke. A man came up the road, saw George and greeted him:

Man: How are you, sir?
George: Not too bad, boy, how's yerself?

The man moved off the road closer to George.

Man: It's a long time since I last saw you, what's the news?
George: Well, me back is not too good, but I'm not too bad all the same.

Man: Same with me, boy, since I got that strain years ago (in the woods), I've never
         been myself.

They continued talking about their health and about woodswork for a while;
then George inquired:

George: Where'r you off to, sir?
Man: I had in my mind to go up to Island Harbour (the neighbouring community) to
         have my hair cut. (Pause) Do you still cut hair like you used to in the woods?
George: Oh yes, the scattered time. (Pause) Come in to the store now, I'll see what I
         can do.

They entered George's store, George got his scissors and began cutting the
man's hair. They chatted all the time about various things: their health, the
shortage of work, the time they used to work in the woods (the man is also
a former logger), about the young people going to Toronto, and other things.
After George finished cutting, the man asked: "Now, how much do you want
for that, sir?" When George replied, "Nothin' sir, nothin'," the man said,
"I'll get you some salt fish – we have some prime in the stage." They continued talking for a while outside the store, and the conversation touched
upon the rising cost of living and welfare payments. Then George invited
the man to go inside the house where conversation turned to welfare regulations and their handling by the welfare officer. The man did not leave before
late afternoon, the visit having lasted several hours.

There is not too much difference between this sequence of interaction and
any other that George may have had with any neighbour. However, it was
especially cordial and supportive and lasted somewhat longer than normal;
it was also unique in that much of the talk revolved around welfare. This is
not surprising considering that the other man was also living off welfare; in
fact, the visitor had been on welfare for most of the year for several years.
While George used to see this man regularly when they were both working,
they have apparently not interacted very much for some time. After the
above visit, however, the man used to come and have a chat with George at
least once a week.

Although George did not establish a close relationship with this man or
any other welfare recipient in the community, he definitely intensified his
interaction with him and a few other recipients since he became unemployed.
This development was due not only to frequent chance encounters but also to
reasons of a more social nature. First, George had a great need "just to talk
to" other men. He often told me that he "felt a bit lonely" and that "he
didn't get around very much"; he found it nice to have me living next door
"to have someone to talk to." Secondly, he needed to talk to other welfare
recipients about things that would be embarrassing to discuss with non-
recipients; namely, matters regarding welfare regulations. These regulations
change continuously (cf. Ch. 2) and many recipients are ill-informed about

them. Information about the regulations seems to be conveyed as much through personal networks among the recipients as through the welfare authorities. George, of course, has a special problem in not being able to read.

Thirdly, interaction with other recipients has less of the defensiveness and asymmetry characterizing interaction between a recipient and a non-recipient. Symmetrical interaction in personal relations is based on the actors' having certain critical attributes in common, and one such attribute among adult men is being able to work for a living. In view of this, a person who is not working and is "on the dole" will be constantly concerned to show that it is not his own fault – that it is not because of unwillingness to work. A welfare recipient accordingly feels continuous pressure, and indeed, may implicitly be requested to defend the fact that he is not working. In interacting with fellow welfare recipients, one does not have to feel this defensive.

Interactions which welfare recipients establish with other recipients are, however, restricted in other respects: they cannot talk freely about their own unique circumstances for being on welfare, which, as we have seen, is one of their main themes of conversation with non-recipients. Discussing it with other recipients would often imply an indirect or direct criticism of other recipients if they should not happen to be in more or less the same situation. Recipients thus have to talk about their shared characteristics. These typically include such items as the low payments, the difficulty of getting employment, and only if their situations are similar, do they include such things as their working careers, their health, their family situations, or the success of their children.

George was thus selective in his assocation with other welfare recipients on more than a casual basis. Significantly, the man in the incident outlined above, as well as the three or four other recipients with whom George had more than a casual relationship, all had several attributes that George had: notably, a long working career as a woodsman and an excuse for not working at present – a bad back.

For a welfare recipient to establish new relations or to intensify old ones with other recipients is likely to lead to difficulties in maintaining his social standing and relationships with non-recipients in his neighbourhood and the community as a whole. George himself seems to be well aware of this. His awareness of the potential negative effects of his interaction with other recipients showed up in his use of the information he got from conversations with them. Several times, I observed George's non-use of information he picked up from other recipients in his conversations with non-recipients, although the information would have been highly relevant. On other occasions, he used the information but did not give the source as is customary; for example, "I talked with a man over at the store this mornin' and he said ..." When the source was a more respected person in the community, he would be cited:

"I saw John Jones down the road this mornin' and he said there were a lot of puffins out in the bay." Also related to this point is the following: after a visit from one of the recipients mentioned earlier, I heard George say to a neighbour who had observed the visit, "That man was a hard worker, a good woodsman until he hurt his back."

George's remark can be interpreted as an explanation – a way of controlling the implications that might be in discord with his social standing (Goffman, 1961:104). He finds such an explanation necessary because other (employed) people in his neighbourhood would not talk positively about this man, but would characterize him as "not very industrious," "somewhat lazy," and his health as "not too bad at all." One reason for this difference of opinion might be that this man lived in a neighbourhood where many men were on welfare (see below) and people in George's neighbourhood did not know him as well as did George.

Even in a small community such as Squid Cove where "everybody knows everybody," people do not know each other equally well. In addition, people tend to forget information they once possessed and use information selectively according to their own positions in the community. George is thus likely to look more favourably on his recipient visitors than his (George's) non-recipient friends and neighbours. More important in this context, while the recipient visitor can be said to belong to George's network of interpersonal relations, he (the visitor) did not belong to the network of any of George's non-recipient friends or neighbours.

The social worth of a welfare recipient in the community cannot then be divorced from his position in the network of interpersonal relations: he is not evaluated purely on the basis of standard or objective criteria which people apply regardless of where that person is situated in their social network. Therefore, not only did many of the recipients (known to a certain informant) become special cases, but different informants would name different people as being special. In several instances, informants possessed intimate knowledge about those they regarded as special cases; and/or the informants belonged to the recipient's network of personal relations.

Recipients, as well as employed men, talked negatively about themselves. George, for instance, told me and other people, "I'm a lot better off than many around here. Some of them are just sittin' there, never tried to get somethin' to do and they haven't worked very much in the past either, and they don't have as big a family to take care of as I have." Significantly, the individuals whom George characterized as "them" did not belong to his social network. By the same token, a non-recipient's reaction to the increase in interaction of a recipient friend with another recipient depends on the latter's position in relation to his own network. Let me clarify this point with several illustrative incidents.

George's friend, William, needed a buddy to go moose hunting and as

George and I were partners that year, he had to look for someone else. He found a man who was also on welfare. George had never interacted very much with this man, but the fact that he had been William's buddy allowed George to see him more after the moose hunt.

On another occasion, George began interacting with a welfare recipient who had worked as a logger for many years. This man did not belong to the personal network of any of George's neighbours, and was referred to by some of them as one "who's always been on welfare." As George's interaction with this man increased, they indicated their disapproval through casual good-natured witticisms about the man. George picked up the clues and saw less of him.

Resentment between an employed man and a welfare recipient can also occur indirectly through a third person or, more generally, through networks of personal relations. This may be illustrated by an actual incident not involving George, but another welfare recipient I shall call John. John had a friend Bill whom he had worked with and who lived in George's neighbourhood. Bill and John used to see one another regularly, although much less after John became unemployed. Bill had another friend, Peter, who was a construction worker and had done well according to local standards by becoming a skilled carpenter. John and Peter did not socialize although they "knew" each other in the way that everyone knows everyone else in Squid Cove. The friendships between Bill and John, and Bill and Peter did not interfere with each other until John went on welfare, or more precisely, began socializing with another man, Robert, who had been on welfare for some time. Bill did not seem to mind; indeed, he did not seem to know about it. Peter, on the other hand, knew Robert since he had to pass his house every day on his way to work, and did not think much of him: "He was never workin', only idlin' around his house all the time. He didn't even clean up around the house; it looked right messy."

Now, Peter had seen John, his friend's friend, visiting Robert several times and he thought they behaved as if they were good buddies. He told Bill about this implying, according to Bill, that he (Bill) should stop socializing with John since he did not keep good company. Bill, however, did not immediately stop seeing John because "he found it difficult." He never told John what Peter had told him, and although Bill and John saw each other after this, their friendship seemed to cool to the extent that Bill never visited John because he thought it might offend Peter.

This example illustrates some of the difficulties a welfare recipient may have in maintaining a friendly relationship with other recipients and non-recipients at the same time, even if he keeps the interaction separate in space and time.

The occasions where social pressure through interpersonal networks is not likely to be exerted, or if exerted, not likely to be effective is when there is an additional relationship besides friendship uniting a person with a recipient: close kin and/or close neighbours, for example. In such cases, if pressure is applied, the man in question would likely argue, "Well, he's my neighbour; we've known each other for years. I can't behave different towards him than I always done." The possibility of excusing the interaction would be greater still if the welfare recipient were a brother or another close relative.

The fact that George resides in a neighbourhood where few of the other men are on welfare and that, in addition, many of his neighbours are close kin acts as a kind of buffer as far as social pressure is concerned. As long as George keeps his interaction with other welfare recipients within certain behavioural limits, socializing with them would not make it difficult for him to maintain good relations within his own neighbourhood.

We can contrast George's situation with that of a welfare recipient, John, who lives in a neighbourhood – let us call it the Bay neighbourhood – where there are several other recipients. John used to be a logger, but about seven years ago he had to give it up because of a bad back which had troubled him for some time. John is in his early fifties, is married, and has five children. His circumstances are thus similar to George's except for the fact that he has a smaller family and he lives in a neighbourhood where there are many other recipients. Three of his next-door neighbours, including one of his two brothers, have been on welfare for some time. Two other neighbours are on medical certificates and, all in all, about a third of the household heads in the Bay are dependent on welfare as their only or major source of income.

When he was employed as a logger, John socialized with both the neighbours who were employed and with those who were on welfare. He also socialized extensively with men from the other neighbourhoods in Squid Cove, especially with his workmates whose homes he visited. When John went on welfare he saw less of his former workmates. Only when he stopped working in the woods did he seem to realize how much of his interaction with his workmates had been related to their common work role. For instance, much of the visiting had been taken up with making arrangements for driving back to the wood camps after a long weekend, for talking over a procedure, wages, and so on. However, the conversation often covered a wider range of topics and it seemed that John and his workmates used their work as an excuse for socializing in a more general way.

However, when John "quit the woods," he did not have any excuses for visiting his former workmates, finding "it difficult to just go and visit them." As time went on and the mechanization process in the woods increased, he also found that he had difficulty in contributing to much of the conversation. He gradually lost interest in the logging business; it was "boring with all the talk about the woods." For all these reasons, John interacted with his former workmates less and less. On the other hand, he came to socialize more with his own neighbours; he spent more time at home now that he did not go away to work and he developed a common interest with them. Like George, he began lobster fishing which many of his neighbours on welfare also engaged in.

As stated previously, showing neighbourliness is highly valued in Newfoundland rural communities. However, when many of the neighbours are welfare recipients, neighbourliness is likely to be looked upon in a different light by people in other neighbourhoods where only "a scattered few" are on welfare. People from the other neighbourhoods in Squid Cove were often heard commenting on the Bay neighbourhood: "They always stick to themselves down there. They seem to prefer each other's company"; or "The one gets the other into it (welfare). Soon everybody will be on welfare down there"; or "They're not even good neighbours down there. They often come and talk bad about each other to us. A good neighbour wouldn't do that, would he?"

John could hardly have not noticed such statements about his neighbourhood, although he argued that he had never heard any of his "friends" saying these things in his presence. At any rate, he does not seem to have taken them too seriously. After he became unemployed, however, he realized that the Bay people did, indeed, largely "stick to themselves." But their reasons for doing so were not those implied by people from other neighbourhoods — that they preferred each other's company. Rather, it was their circumstances and the attitudes of people from the other neighbourhoods who forced them to restrict themselves to fellow recipients.

The Bay neighbourhood is situated about half a mile from the centre of Squid Cove where the main shops, the school, the doctor's residence, the public wharf, and other public places are found. To get to them, the Bay people have to pass through the other neighbourhoods. Having no specific task to perform in these public places (even when they have one, they say "who would know when they see you walkin' on the road?"), *and* residing in the Bay *and* being on welfare make Bay people hesitate to use these places. In John's words, "If a workin' man is idlin' around up there, it's a very different matter than if a man on welfare is doin' so. The workin' man is only relaxin' from his work which a hard workin' man deserves; the man on welfare, idlin' around, is remindin' the others that he is idle — not workin,' that is."

I observed George experience this problem on several occasions, but to a lesser extent than the men on welfare from the Bay neighbourhood. When George, for instance, went to the shop several times a day, this did not draw any comments from working people to the effect that he was idling around because he lived only a couple of hundred yards from the shop. For a man from the Bay neighbourhood to visit the shop more than once a day would be commented on and considered "foolish," since he had half a mile to walk.

An illustration might show why people conclude that the Bay people "stick to themselves." One Saturday morning, John stood talking to a logger on the community wharf in Squid Cove. They had both been out fishing and had met casually on the wharf. John and this man had never interacted regularly but knew each other from the time both worked as loggers. The conversation focused on fishing: the better places to fish, what equipment gave the better catch, how to keep up the boats, and the like. The conversation was rather friendly and egalitarian and both seemed to be interested in what the other had to say. The information exchanged would be of some use to both on future fishing trips (cf. Ch. 6 and the common sub-culture). Shortly after, another man, also a welfare recipient and a neighbour of John's joined the conversation which continued to be about fishing, and in the course of which the working man and the newly arrived welfare recipient got into a trivial argument on how best to keep up boats. The working man appealed to John for support for his statements saying: "Now, John what do you think?" John replied that he thought his neighbour was right, and the argument continued with the two welfare recipients teaming up against the working man. The working man tried several times to get John to give support to his own statements. "But John, you just said earlier ... ," whereupon John replied, "Well, that wasn't exactly what I meant. I said that ..." After a short while, the working man left, somewhat irritated. Afterwards, he said to me: "You can never trust those men (the welfare recipients from the Bay); they always stick together. Don't never get into an argument with two of them at a time." John, commenting on the incident later told me that "They (the working men) always want to be right. They thinks they're so much better than we because we're out of work."

Sometimes the 'alignment' may be different; that is, John would team up with a working man. Once, I observed an encounter in which John and a neighbour, also on welfare, were passing the house of one of John's former workmates. The latter was engaged in some heavy work on his house and John and the neighbour stopped to chat with him. After some time, John offered to help and asked his neighbour to join. The neighbour excused himself saying that he had some work to do at home and left. John helped his former workmate for an hour or so. After they finished the job, his workmate remarked on John's neighbour's hurry to leave without helping. John replied, "Well, I guess he can't stay away from his wife too long," and both men had a good laugh, since the man was known to be rather jealous. John's friend later commented on this incident saying, "That man (John's former workmate) wouldn't have asked us to give him a hand if we hadn't been on welfare. They think they can ask a man for any kind of service just because he's out of work: they think we're just idlin' around all the time." To this John replied, "Well, I guess you're right, they do. But

I used to do work with this man in the woods years ago. I had to offer him a hand. Anyway he didn't say nothin' when you said you had no time to give him a hand."

This incident shows some interesting differences in interpretation between two men experiencing the same situation. While John's neighbour felt that he and John were *asked* to "give a hand," John (and I, as an observer) felt that he *offered* to help. I am inclined to see the reason for this difference as being the different relationship which John and his neighbour had to the employed man; being a former workmate of his, John gave the most positive interpretation. Also, John having been on welfare for a shorter time than his neighbour, seemed to be more confident in being able to maintain a cordial relationship with employed men in general. I shall have more to say about the problems of being on good terms with 'both sides,' later.

At this stage, I would like to draw attention to a characteristic aspect of the relations between employed men and welfare recipients. What the above encounters show clearly is how the statuses of the employed on the one hand, and the unemployed and welfare recipients on the other, are being used to explain a wide variety of behaviour and motivations by the employed as well as by the welfare recipients. In this way, the work statuses tend to be used as explanations for most interactions and, hence, act to polarize the employed and unemployed.

The use of such collective statuses to explain a variety of types of behaviour seems to contrast with how, for instance, employed and welfare recipients explain behaviour they dislike among themselves. I never heard, for instance, behavioural quirks attributed to "those loggers" or "those construction workers"; rather, one would blame the personality, saying, for example, that "Jack Jones has always been like that; already when he was a child he ..."; or one would blame the family: "Those Jones have always been smart"; or the community or neighbourhood: "Those people from X Cove have always been peculiar." Yet, in the above cases, the collective statuses attached to unemployment and neighbourhood tend to merge.

When John first became unemployed and had to go on welfare, he tried to maintain relations on both sides; that is, to socialize with his employed friends as well as his neighbours on welfare. Some of his difficulties in doing so have been analysed above, with special reference to the fact that he lived in the Bay neighbourhood. There are still other difficulties not directly related to his place of residence but which often become conceived as a consequence of living there by people from other neighbourhoods. One such difficulty is apparent from the last incident recorded above: that John finds himself giving different impressions about his loyalties to his former workmate and to his welfare recipient neighbour.

A welfare recipient who socializes with other recipients as well as with non-recipients often finds himself involved in, what one may call double-talk. With other recipients, he talks mostly about their common fate and about non-recipients "who think they are so much better." With non-recipients, he talks about his unique circumstances for being on welfare and about the negative attributes of other recipients, including his neighbours. Making derogatory comments about other recipients is, one can easily see, one way of dissociating oneself from one's neighbourhood. Such double-talk would have few or no consequences on the relationship between neighbourhoods if they were completely isolated. However, we have seen that there are a number of interpersonal relationships criss-crossing the neighbourhoods, although they are becoming fewer and fewer (see below). Also, Squid Cove is a small community with closely knit networks of interpersonal relations (Barnes, 1954), and people, in time, become aware of such double-talk.

If and when a recipient is caught double-talking, it could be very damaging to the recipient's social standing among the non-recipients as well as among other recipients. Non-recipients seem to be especially willing to regard such behaviour as dishonest and as a negative personality characteristic independent of the social context which gave rise to it. Cause and effect are thus easily confused; people would say "you can't trust him; one day he says this and the next that. No wonder he don't get a job."

Many welfare recipients from the Bay did not seem to ascribe such behaviour to personality but rather to a "fact of life." The consequence of such a view of life seems to be that stable and trusting interpersonal relations outside the immediate family are difficult to maintain in a welfare neighbourhood. Relationships thus tend to fluctuate more than in other neighbourhoods.

People from the other neighbourhoods found the style of communication used by many of the Bay people aggressive, also. It is probable that much of this aggressiveness is due to a feeling among the welfare recipients that their welfare status was made to count where it should not. For example, a woman from the Bay neighbourhood, whose husband was on welfare, wanted to visit a relative in another community. There were no taxis available at the time and she went to see a young man whom she knew used to do some taxiing. The conversation ran approximately as follows:

Woman: You shouldn't be goin' to ... Cove this evening?
Young man: I don't think so – I might, though, later.
Woman: You understand, I was goin' to see me sister's and the taxi man is gone
           to ... town and he won't be back before tomorrow.
Young man: Well, I wouldn't know – I promised to do a few things for me dad and ...
Woman: Me sister's sick you see and she phoned me and asked me if I could come
           over (and more details about her sister).
Young man: Well, I don't know ...
Woman: I can pay you now if you like.
Young man (after a pause): O.K. then I'll drive you.

To an urban outsider, this woman might not appear aggressive enough and her method was not apparent to the ethnographer either, until he learned the outport style of asking a favour. One does not ask directly "would you do this for me?" Rather, one introduces one's request by implication which could be understood as a wish *or* as a neutral remark. In this way, one succeeds in getting an indication from the questioned of his disposition but at the same time, not putting him in a situation in which he has to refuse outright. If the questioned indicated some reluctance in his reply, one would stop the inquiry and leave it at that. On the other hand, if he indicated willingness, one would take this as a message allowing one to continue to be more specific about one's wish and eventually perhaps ask outright if an agreement had not already been arrived at through the indirect way. During these exchanges, an agreement about the payment or price might also be reached, but more often, this is not done until the transaction is completed. The questioned may refuse financial payment and this may be accepted by the initiator; instead, he may promise to return the favour in some way.

From this analysis, it should be clear that the woman who wanted the young man to drive her broke these unwritten rules first by pressing the man after he had indicated his reluctance from the start, and secondly, by her last statement: "I can pay." For our present purpose, the last statement is the most critical, in that the woman shows that she has misinterpreted or at least not accepted the young man's stated reasons for his unwillingness to drive her. Presumably, she thought that the man refused her because she was from the "Bay" and on welfare, and therefore was either not in a position and/or was unwilling to pay for the taxi; that is, the statuses of the unemployed and the welfare recipient (her husband) were crucial factors in the transaction. Later, this young man told me when I inquired (indirectly) about the incident (which I had overheard), "Those people never think you're telling the truth and they always press you. They're right forceful." Hence, the incident reinforced his negative view of welfare recipients.

Such encounters also give rise to a special type of double-talk. The woman probably told her friends and neighbours that the young man was lying when he first said he had no time to drive her. The real reason for his reluctance, she would say, was because he was not sure he would be paid; and his reason for finally driving her was because she told him that she would pay – proof of her interpretation. The young man, on the other hand, told me that his main reason for giving in was because he thought the woman would not give up until he agreed to drive her. Moreover, he did not believe that her sister was really sick, but he did not want to argue and make an issue of it. He pretended he believed the woman but told his friends and neighbours that he really did not believe her.

Incidents such as the one reported above take place in a variety of situations between the employed and welfare recipients. It is perhaps most critical in encounters where services are exchanged, but one can find the same antagonism developing where the exchange is verbal only, as in descriptive accounts of a local event or person. In these conversations, the slightest indication – or rather the recipient's interpretation as such – of discrimination on behalf of the employed, may lead a recipient to break with the style of outport communication and as a result, be regarded as aggressive by the unemployed. Indeed, some recipients, especially the younger ones (cf. Ch. 9), seem to have adopted a new style altogether, in that they drop the typical outport caution and indirectness in initiating a conversation. Two brothers in their early twenties, both unemployed, would begin a conversation by stating, for example, "I (we) got a good catch of fish this mornin' ..." Other Squid Cove men, young as well as old, employed as well as unemployed, would typically start such an account by saying "I was out fishin' today ..." and then leave it up to the listeners to ask for details.

Similarly, the brothers often initiated a conversation by asking: "I saw you were out fishin' today. How much did you get?" The outport style is something like, "I saw you were out fishin' today; the sea looked smooth," and then leave it to the man to lead the conversation in the direction he wanted, asking about the catch only if the man indicated that he wanted to be asked that question. The two brothers would generally be regarded as aggressive and boastful and imposing themselves upon others. To some extent, however, they were regarded as special cases, and although they were both on welfare and from the Bay neighbourhood, people did not regard their behaviour as being typical of Bay people, but rather of the younger generation (cf. Ch. 9). On the other hand, as regards aggressiveness, there was a tendency to generalize in the same way the young taxi-driver did about the Bay woman referred to above.

The point that I want to stress at this stage, then, is that although people from the other neighbourhood may regard the Bay people as individuals (some of them are worse than others), they also generalize about the neighbourhood as such. This is perhaps most obvious in the statements about the spreading of welfare in the Bay. If there are a number of welfare recipients in one neighbourhood and fewer, or "only the scatter one" in other neighbourhoods, then this situation is ascribed by the people from the latter neighbourhoods to internal factors; that is, in the former neighbourhood, one man on welfare is thought to sway his neighbour over to his way of life. The major evidence for such a process is the fact that "they always stick together," implying that they have a bad influence on each other. Many people also argue that welfare "seems to be in the family." A common statement among working men is that when one Jones applies for welfare, he entices his brother to apply and they, in turn, entice their cousin and then they marry and get their in-laws into it. Noting that near kin often settle close to each other in the outports, one can see that the statements about "going in the family" and "going in the neighbourhood" often mean the same thing.

Furthermore, such statements emphasize possible negative personal, family, or neighbourhood characteristics in contrast to characteristics outside the control of any of these units; namely, the state of the labour market in Newfoundland where work is indeed, scarce. Yet, there is certainly a relationship between family and neighbourhood, and the labour market. First of all, as has been indicated previously, work in rural Newfoundland is often found through personal networks rather than through employment agencies or through formal training. This situation is due to the fact that much of the work in rural Newfoundland such as fishing, logging, construction, and road work, is work which most men can perform with some on-the-job training. Proper connections rather than special skills are often the most crucial asset in getting work, the most important being those based on kinship and neighbourhood. A man looking for work, whose kin and neighbours are also without work, is thus greatly handicapped in the competition for jobs.

A difference in emphasis shows up in other respects, also. While people from other neighbourhoods often state that the Bay people "have always been like that" (on welfare), the Bay people themselves emphasize the personal history of their neighbours. John, for instance, would tell me he felt that most of his neighbours had good excuses for being on welfare. Two of them were over fifty years of age and had been working in the woods for twenty-five years; they were not in the best of health, although not sick enough to get medical certificates. A third neighbour, aged forty, had worked in the woods for sixteen years and had been laid off because the labour force had been reduced. Several others who were now living mainly off welfare had worked on and off various construction jobs. When the roads in the area were completed and mechanization in this field cut down the work force, these men found it difficult to find work. They could not work as loggers because of their limited experience in the woods and because of the extensive cut-back in the labour force. The only alternative open to them, said John, would be to move to the mainland (Canada). But finding a job on the mainland would be difficult because of their lack of skills and their low educational standard and also because they had no relatives there to help them through the initial stages.

The point I would like to stress in this context is how the occupational careers of welfare recipients are often forgotten. Many recipients have been on welfare for a long time, but before they went on welfare they had worked many years, the older men especially. Unless such men belong to one's own personal network and/or to one's own neighbourhood, people seem to forget this, and make remarks such as "he's never been working as far back as I can remember." The younger members of the community are perhaps more correct in saying this, since it may be that some men have not had any regular employment "as far back as they can remember."

An unintentional manifestation of another discrepancy is the following. I hired a research assistant for a short time to complete a census of Squid

Cove after I had left the community. The assistant, aged twenty-five, had lived all his life in the community except for spending three years at the university in St. John's; he had also taught locally for two or three years. His knowledge of the community, therefore, should have been trustworthy and he was, indeed, chosen for that reason. One of the questions he was to research, according to his own estimations, was the condition of health for every household head. After the census was completed, I found that he had written "excellent health" about a couple of men whom I happened to know rather well and whose health was far from excellent. I then checked all my assistant's statements with the local doctor who knew most of the men. The two statements showed a significant discrepancy: for 25 per cent (9 out of 47) of the men whose health my assistant specified as excellent, the doctor classified as "not too good" or "poor."

A final point which was often overlooked by people from other neighbourhoods when they ascribed the spread of welfare in the Bay area to internal causes is that the concentration of welfare families in the neighbourhood is partly due to selective processes of in- and out-migration. People who, in one way or another, are able to keep their jobs while many of their neighbours and kin cannot, are likely to feel pressure to move out of the neighbourhood. I recorded six families who moved out of the Bay neighbourhood in the last few years. On the other hand, some families already on welfare moved into the neighbourhood; in these cases, the change of residence was related to the marriage of a girl from the Bay neighbourhood to a boy from a neighbourhood or community with little welfare. The outport custom is for a newlywed couple to settle in the boy's natal community. However, if the boy becomes unemployed and has to apply for welfare, and be the only one in his community or in his family to experience this "disgrace," there would be a strong motive to move to the Bay community where he would not be alone. I registered four such changes of residence to the Bay and several more to other 'welfare' communities. It could be added that such changes of residence connected with marriage adds to the native theory that welfare 'is in the family' and that girls are also affected.

The several processes with which we have been dealing in the second part of this chapter can be summarized as ghettorization. In the most general sense, ghettorization implies the spacial and social isolation of a category of people having significant attributes in common, typically ethnic attributes but in our case, those of being unemployed and living on welfare. The process in our case seems to have been initiated by the fact that several men in one neighbourhood became unemployed and had difficulties in getting new jobs, while in the other neighbourhoods, people managed to maintain their jobs or acquire new jobs, notably in construction. The difference in ability to gain new types of employment was largely due to social networks, but has been interpreted as due to differences in character – in one's willingness to work and initiative. In addition, the concentration of unemployed welfare recipients in one neighbourhood was looked upon as being caused by internal dynamics in the neighbourhood (one man enticed another to go on welfare), rather than by the general scarcity of work in Newfoundland. This interpretation has been reinforced by the fact that several men from the same (extended) family went on welfare. Welfare, then, "goes" not only in the neighbourhood, but also in various families. As mentioned above, the settling of welfare recipients in one neighbourhood in Squid Cove has also been encouraged by selective out- and in-migration.

The status difference between a welfare recipient and an employed person now pervades most types of interaction as the Bay neighbourhood becomes increasingly identified as a welfare community. This factor, in turn, has led to fewer interpersonal relations cutting across the neighbourhoods. The imputation of a wide range of imperfections on the basis of the original one, unemployment, seems to be directly related to the decrease in such crosscutting relations. We may thus conclude that the ghettorization process is largely caused by the outside; that is, by the selective interpretation and emphasis of available information by people from the other neighbourhoods in the community.

One social process remains to be analysed; namely, the effect of welfare over the generations. This will be the subject of the following chapter.

Although the older children have left home and have done fairly well, George and Elizabeth are concerned with what the future will bring for the rest of their children. Elizabeth especially, often made comments such as: "I hope the children will get their education. You need so much education now to get some work. The older ones didn't get too much, but they done well all the same."

George, on the other hand, would often contrast his children's better opportunities with his own, and one can feel some ambivalence in his attitude towards education. "I never got no learnin'; I had to go work when I was thirteen. Take David now, he's eighteen; that's five years older than I was when I first went to work. I don't think he'd be able to do the work I did, but he's got his education (grade 11). He won't end up with a chain-saw (that is, become a logger) and I give him credit for that."

The younger children have come to look at education as the way to get ahead. Edward, aged twelve, who has done well in school so far says, "I wants every education I can get. If you don't get education you don't get jobs — then you have to work in the woods. I wants to be a policeman. I wants to be a policeman in a big city." In contrast, his brother John, aged sixteen, dislikes going to school. One reason for this might be that he has not done too well, and also would prefer to start working and join his older brothers in Toronto. Elizabeth and George, however, both think he is too young to go to Toronto and that "he needs all the education he can get before he goes."

David, aged eighteen, having done well at school, also wanted to quit several times. George explains, "David is in grade 11 now, but if it hadn't been for we, he would have quit and gone to Toronto." In fact, as soon as the final exams were over, and before the results were known, David and three of his friends went to Toronto to look for work. Boys from low-income outport families, even if they are relatively successful at school and like it, seem to experience a conflict between continuing their education and starting to earn money when they reach the age of sixteen to eighteen. The conflict between education and work does not seem to be as strong for girls, although this seems to have been so for George's three oldest girls who all went to work at an early age, partly to help their family.

Ann, aged fourteen, who has not been doing well at school — in fact, she had to repeat her last two grades — still wants to continue. Indeed, she seems to be the most determined of all the children. "I don't want to quit school, that's for sure. I'll never quit school." Besides "wanting her education," she has two other important reasons for not quitting. First, she is, in fact, "working" at present being her mother's helper and highly regarded in that capacity (see Ch. 5). Secondly, her closest friends, both first cousins, are very interested in school and plan to go to "secretary school" when they finish high school. Moreover, her older sister Janet, aged twenty-one, who quit school in grade 9 (and went to Toronto with one of her married sisters, but has been home for the last two years) now regrets not finishing her high school education. "Sometimes I dream about it at night. I wish I hadn't quit. If I go to Toronto again, I'm going to evenin' school for sure." Ann, as well as her friends, seems to look up to Janet who is an attractive and popular girl. Although I never heard Janet advise her sister about going to school, there is little doubt that Ann has been influenced by the fact that her sister talked about her regrets so often.

From these observations it is possible to isolate at least four factors which influence the children in their attitude towards school. First, they are more inclined to continue their education if they are successful. It should be noted that success at school is believed to be achieved more by innate qualities than by hard work (cf. Ch. 1 and George's remark "I was never any good at learnin' "). The attitude is, perhaps, fatalistic (Kitchen, 1969), but this fatalism has a practical component: it reinforces the egalitarian values in outport culture. Nobody is looked down upon because he does not do well in school. This may, however, be changing at present with many outports adopting more urban middle-class values.

Secondly, the attitude is influenced by the view held by one's peers, particularly by one's best friends. This influence is especially strong among teenagers – a fact which partially accounts for the members of one family having different views on education: John had a first cousin among his closest friends who had a negative view of education, while David's closest friend was another first cousin who, although he did not like going to school, was literate and had been living in Montreal for some years. I had a feeling that David's success at school was partly determined by his eagerness to equal his friend. Janet's regrets about not finishing school seem largely influenced by the fact that her present circle of friends include the younger teachers in the community; in addition, some of her closest friends have married local teachers.

A third factor is parental influence. Outport parents in general, do not pressure their children to go to school to the extent that this is done in Western, urban, middle-class cultures. The reasons for this are related to their fatalistic view of the ability to learn, to their treatment of teenagers as adults more than children, and to the financial strain of keeping children in school – not only with regard to the family budget, but also to the potential income that teenagers could add to the family purse if they were working.

Older siblings may influence their younger brothers and sisters more than the parents. There also seems to be more pressure within families that are occupationally mobile, and have, what is regarded in the outport settings as middle-class jobs, although these occupations would be working-class in an urban area (for example, skilled construction jobs). Their attitude towards education typifies that held by occupationally mobile people: if one has initiative and works hard, one can always get ahead.

A final factor is the teenagers' own concern with not being a drain, but rather a contributor to the family income. This is especially so in larger families where what some children get, others have to do without; for example, those going to high school need more expensive clothing (cf. Ch. 2). This is recognized by the parents and pressure is exerted by school mates, especially at the high school where there are children from families who are better off financially and who can afford to dress their children well. Children of poorer families cannot ask their parents for more and better clothing, and so they have to earn the money for it themselves. David, for instance, travelled to all the major centres in the province to get a summer job. The fact that he was unsuccessful upset him very much and this seemed to be one of the reasons why he wanted to quit school and go to Toronto (and hence his eagerness [cf. Ch. 6] to sell subsistence goods to the neighbours).

The basic question to be asked in this context is to what extent a family's being on welfare influences the school performances of the children. Most studies seem to agree that "by every conceivable measure, children of low-income families do not do as well in school as children from more affluent ones" (Goldstein, 1967:31). For Newfoundland, Kitchen (1969) reports a high correlation between low school performance on one hand, and residence in small communities, illiterate parents, low family incomes, and large families on the other. However, rather than family background, the major explanation for the lower level of achievement among youth from small outports has been the lower standard of education in these communities: one- or two-room schools and teachers with little training. This is manifested in areas where integrated high schools have been established.[1]

1   Newfoundland has a denominational system of education, each faith (Anglican, Roman Catholic, United Church, Salvation Army, and Pentecostal) building and maintaining its own schools, both elementary and secondary, with the help of grants from the provincial government. However, one curriculum serves all schools. In communities or clusters of communities where all the denominations are represented and have a population size which can support a school, there may be as many as five elementary schools. The denominational system has resulted in a proliferation of small schools and most outports have at least two. (Squid Cove has one United Church and one Pentecostal school.) In the last decade or so, most newly built schools have been

It is also postulated that lower achievement among youth from low-income and welfare families is due to a lower level of aspiration. It is argued that the youth from low-income families do not value education as highly nor do they aspire to as much education as youth from more fortunate backgrounds (Goldstein, 1967; Kitchen 1969). This may well be so. I did not obtain specific enough data to be able to support or reject these arguments. The data I did gather on the subject, however, did not confirm the low aspiration hypothesis. There were a number of children from welfare families who performed above average in school, while conversely, there were children from working and middle-class families whose performance was rather poor. Also, as we have seen, there can be significant differences within a single family.

Such differences can perhaps be explained by differences in ability or IQ, and a feasible generalization would thus be that for children with the same IQ, those from more affluent families would have a better chance to realize their potentials. However, it seems that it is not isolated factors such as illiterate parents, family on welfare, or large family *per se*, that cause lower performances at school. Indeed, illiterate parents (or parent) in some cases show a greater interest in their children's education than the literate because they have experienced such deprivation themselves.

Also, in some cases, coming from a large family was an asset rather than a drawback, at least for the younger children. In several families I became acquainted with, the older siblings encouraged verbally, as well as financially, their younger siblings to go to school. This was often recognized by the younger siblings: several told me that "if it hadn't been for my older brother(s) (sister), I would never have finished high school." In one case in Squid Cove, I heard of an older brother (working in Toronto) sending his younger sister a one hundred dollar reward when she completed grade 9 and she expected to "get even more" when she completed grade 10.

Even being on welfare may act as an incentive for the parents as well as for the children to get more education. For instance, the father's being at home all the time gives him the opportunity to encourage his children more. Also, it seems probable that some men who have been forced to go on welfare and who have experienced the deprivation of not having enough schooling, would put more emphasis on their children doing well. Indeed, the first youth from Squid Cove to ever successfully complete grade 11 came from a family who had been on and off welfare for some time. One man living in the Bay neighbourhood who had been on welfare for many years and who had a rather low status in the community found his main reserve

---

integrated; that is, encompassing all the denominations, particularly the Anglican, United Church, and Salvation Army. (For further information on the denominational system, see Rowe, 1964.)

of self-esteem in one of his sons who was doing, and was being encouraged to do, well in school.

There is no doubt, however, that children from families on welfare are handicapped in school compared to children from working families. This is not always because of internal family processes but rather because of the negative view that the community has of welfare families. Some children from welfare families who have a low standing in the community told me that they "hated the school," their reason being that they felt that some of the other children looked down on them, even if they did not say anything. They also felt that some of the teachers did the same. This need not necessarily have been the case, but the fact remains that the children imagined it to be so.

The cases of "discrimination" they told me about could have been caused by other legitimate reasons. Many teachers have difficulty in communicating with children and youth from low-income and welfare families and are unable to take account of their vulnerability in the class-room setting. Because of this, the teachers may unwittingly concentrate their attention on the youth with whom they have less difficulty in interacting. Also, the school curriculums are oriented toward middle-class values and settings. Children from welfare families are made aware, even if indirectly, that many of the things they bring with them from home are not good enough and that their homes lack many of the items found in a middle-class home.

I was not able to make any comprehensive statistical comparisons on the school performances of children from welfare families and those from families not on welfare; but from the data I collected, I could find no significant differences. On the other hand, the school drop-out rate for outport children in general seems high. Data gathered from one integrated high school attended by the Squid Cove children and by a dozen other neighbouring communities showed that of the 308 boys and girls who went to the school between 1963 and 1968, only 90 passed their grade 11 examinations (grade 11 being the final grade in Newfoundland high schools). Of the 218 who dropped out before grade 11, 143 or close to 50 per cent did not even pass grade 9.

What happens to the drop-outs? With the help of several high school students and teachers, I was able to trace the present (1969) occupations of all the 308 students, and the findings showed that more than 40 per cent of the boys who dropped out were unemployed. For the girls, the unemployment figure was only 10 per cent, but then about 50 per cent of the girls had married and I was not able to get reliable figures about the employment situation of their husbands. I assume, however, that some of these husbands were also unemployed. Still, the girls seem to have had better luck than the boys, partly, I suggest, because they married boys who were older than themselves and who had secured work in a period when the employment situation was better.

The data also showed a drastic increase in the unemployment rate of the drop-outs in the last three years (1965–68). During this period, 5 of the 29 who passed grade 11 were also without work. This increase might, of course, be attributed to the fact that the 1963–65 drop-outs had more time to find a job than the 1966–68 drop-outs. To investigate the effect of this time factor, I traced the employment career of the currently unemployed drop-outs. The data showed that a substantial number, 38 out of 49, had had some employment in the past, a fact suggesting that it is the increasing difficulty to get work rather than the time factor which is the cause of the rise in unemployment. Much of this unemployment is not officially registered because many teenagers (and more girls than boys) live with their parents and do odd jobs within the household as well as pick up what casual employment they can get. They do not generally register with an employment or welfare official, trying instead to get work through personal appeals to employers, some of whom hire more employees than they really need in order to accommodate the teenagers – but then only for short periods of time.

Besides the increase in unemployment among the outport youth, the most significant change in their adaptation, which came out of the high school data, was their moving to mainland Canada (see also Ch. 1). Of the 92 drop-outs during 1963–65, 13 went to the mainland; of the 116 drop-outs during 1966–68, 22 emigrated. Counting only the boys during the last period, about one in every four went to the mainland. Even with this increase in out-migration, there has been a drastic increase in unemployment during the same period.

The figures given above should serve to emphasize the extent of unemployment among the young people. Let us now examine the efforts to obtain work and other facts which lie behind the figures, using the 'careers' of George's two oldest sons as illustrations. They may be regarded as rather typical of outport boys from low income families. Both Eric and Tony dropped out in grade 9 at sixteen years of age when they began working in the woods (see Ch. 2). Eric worked in the woods continuously for six years, and Tony for five, from May to November. Relative to their age and the pay rates in the logging industry, they each made "good money" – between $1,500 and $2,000 during a season. They both found the work hard, however, especially Tony. Although he was the better wood-cutter, he became dissatisfied after a time partly because his best friend, a first cousin who had worked with him, left for Toronto and found Toronto "game".

In the fall of 1967, when Tony went home for a weekend, his sister, brother-in-law and their children were about to leave for Toronto. He decided to join them. The decision was taken on a Sunday and they left Monday morning. In Toronto, he boarded with his sister and shortly after his arrival, got work in a factory. After less than a year, he had a take-home pay of ninety-five dollars a week, and ample opportunity to work overtime.

Tony came home for a visit the following summer and when he left a few weeks later, his older brother Eric, who was unemployed at the time, went with him. Eric had continued working in the woods after his brother left, but because he had not kept up his union fees, he was unable to secure work there the next spring.[2] He got a job in a fish plant fifteen miles from his home community later that spring, but quit after two weeks. He did not like to work inside and the smell in the plant made him sick. In addition, the pay ($1.30 per hour) was less than he earned in the woods, and furthermore, he had to pay board of sixteen dollars per week.

In Toronto, they each boarded with one of their sisters, and Tony helped his brother find a job a couple of days after they arrived. However, Eric did not like living in Toronto. When I visited them in November, Eric declared, "I'll never be able to stay here. I belong back there (in Squid Cove). I'm not made for up here." In April of the next year, Eric quit his job and went back home. He was then paid $2.00 an hour and made between $75 and $90 per week, and had about $400 in savings. He then went seal hunting, something he had been looking forward to all winter. Later in the spring, he went lobster fishing with his father, but the lobster being "wonderful scarce" and not enough work for two men, he quit after a couple of weeks. He then hired himself out as a "shareman" for the trap fishery on the "Straits" (the Straits of Belle Isle, a distance of 300 miles from Squid Cove) together with several of his peers in the community. His two younger brothers, David and John, took his place fishing lobster with their father.

The fishery on the Straits was not successful. In Eric's words, "We didn't get too much fish, but we had a very good time up there. There were parties and dances all the time and plenty of girls." After the trap fishery was over, he came home again and went fishing with George's sister's husband who lives in a neighbouring community and owns a longliner (a type of fishing boat). A berth had just become vacant when another uncle (his father's sister's husband) went to Toronto with his family. While he was fishing with his uncle, Eric made about $75 per week – about as much as he made in Toronto – but in late August, the catches began to decline and the crew was reduced to three men. Eric found himself without work once again.

He then tried to get a job in the woods, going to the head office twice (one hundred miles from Squid Cove), but with no success. He talked about going back to Toronto, but having a fair hope that he would get work in the woods later in the fall, he decided against it. However, he was not able to secure any employment at all during the fall. This is not to say that he did not work; he helped his father cut the firewood for their own use and also for sale to others. He also engaged in various subsistence activities, fishing,

2 The paper companies made an arrangement with the unions the previous year to give preference to union members.

and hunting. However, for much of the fall, he felt he had "nothing to do" and was very restless. "It's the first time since I quit school I haven't had anything to do for this long. I'm almost ashamed stayin' home not workin'." Finally, in January, he "got a chance in the woods." The circumstances surrounding this is perhaps worth recording.

Because of bad weather conditions, a number of loggers were laid off in early December and became liable for unemployment insurance immediately. Some of them did not go back when the logging operations resumed in January, thereby causing a shortage of manpower among union members. Therefore, the company had to hire non-unionized loggers such as Eric. By paying $35 retroactive in union fees, Eric was able to work in the woods until the operation ceased again in March. Then he was without work again, and when I last talked to him, he was not sure if he would be able to get work in the woods again. "I hope I'll get a message when they start loggin' again. If I do, I'll go back into the woods. I liked it last time. It wasn't too hard with all the machinery and we made good money. If I don't get a message, I think I'll go back to Toronto. But they say that work is scarce up there now. I've talked to several fellows that have had to come home because they were laid off."

There seems to be no doubt that Eric would prefer to stay home rather than go to work in Toronto, even if it meant lower pay and that he had to go back to the woods. Tony, on the other hand, seems to have settled down in Toronto. This is also the feeling of his family. In Elizabeth's words, "I think that Tony won't come back now. He don't mind stayin' up there and now he's met this girl. I think they may get married this summer. Tony's different from Eric. Eric is not made for Toronto." When I asked Eric why he and his brother felt so differently about Toronto, he said, "Well, I'm not the type to like it up there. I like fishin', sealin', and huntin'. Tony and Roy (their first cousin) never did much fishin' and huntin' when they were home. They don't like that so much." Eric also knew who among his own friends might like it in Toronto. "Fred is the type that might like it up there. He's clever with girls and he's been around a lot. He can make friends with everybody." In fact, Fred tried to persuade Eric to go to Toronto with him last fall when they could not find any work in the province. Fred was very eager. "If Eric says we go tomorrow, we'll go." But Eric was reluctant. It should be noted that Fred had no kin or friends in Ontario and would not go alone.

As we have seen, Eric had great difficulty in finding a stable job at home and his only chance seems to have been the woods; yet, there was no security there, either. He has been thinking about other types of employment, and fishing in particular. After he had fished on his uncle's longliner, he talked enthusiastically about trying to get himself a boat. "I'd like to have my own outfit. But I have no money. The engine alone costs $1,000 and then I would to have plenty of nets. Me and the old man (his father) could maybe

fish together, though. We wouldn't need so much then. But we couldn't fish
out of here. We would have to fish out of ... Cove or ... Cove. If we had
a good boat, we could sleep in her. It's a risk. though. The fish might not
be as plentiful next year, as this year."

For George to start fishing full-time would presumably be too difficult,
especially since he had no experience with longliners. However, his major
limitation was the capital required. Eric might have saved some money but,
"Eric is not the kind of guy who keeps a dollar. He uses all the money he
earns. If none of his buddies have any money and Eric has some, he'll pay
for them. If he'd put some of the money he's earned in the bank, he'd had
a house now. I've often told him that he should save – he could have had
that (fishing) outfit now. If he wanted to get married now, he's got nothing
of his own."

Eric's and Tony's difficulty in settling down to a particular job, and their
pattern of horizontal mobility is typical for outport boys who have dropped
out of school. It would be wrong to ascribe this to any form of personal
disorganization. Rather, the eagerness to "have a go" at different types of
work may be seen as having an important function for a youth in finding
a work-setting which fits his personality. Another factor in this mobility is
a certain restlessness among youth partly caused by the opening up of the
outport communities, a post-Confederation development (that is, after
1949). At the same time, it is the seasonality and the lack of job opportunities which make possible and encourage the high rate of horizontal mobility.
These factors, along with the kinds of employment which are open to youth
without a high school diploma, make it very difficult to develop, in Goffman's terms (1961), either "commitment" or "attachment" to a particular
job (cf. Goffman, 1961:88–90; see also Stebbins, 1970:526–29).

With regard to commitment, the youth are not greatly constrained by
family responsibilities, and by living in their natal home, they do not need
a great income to maintain a fair standard of living. It should be noted, however, that their need for cash is constantly increasing. A bigger wage does
not go into savings, but is spent on clothes, sports equipment, and pocket
money for spending in the restaurants and dance halls which have been
established in many outport communities in the last few years.

The greatest expenditure seems to be on cars. All boys do not own cars;
in fact only a minority do. However, most have a friend with a car and share
the expenses of gasoline and repairs when they take a trip together. Not
having a car becomes critical only when one does not have a friend with one,
or when one begins to date a girl seriously and it becomes less desirable to
"stay with the boys." For young boys who have a car, it is extremely difficult
to give it up. The car plays an important part in giving them an identity.
By doing most of the repair work themselves (all the roads in the area

are dirt roads and in poor condition), they are able to keep a car even with a low income. A twenty-two year-old boy, working seasonally at his father's sawmill had this to say: "If you've got some money and a car, you can have as much fun around here as anywhere else. But if you haven't got any money, you'll have no fun at all. Workin' for the old man just keeps me goin' with beer and the car. I wouldn't know what to do without the car. I wouldn't get nowhere – would have to stay home all the time."

In this type of youth culture, what seems to be important to the boy is not the *kind* of work he has; one's popularity is not dependent on the type of job or how long one keeps a job, but rather, whether one is able to get work at all. In this sense, Eric and Tony for instance, have been fortunate compared to many other boys in their own age group as well as to youngsters who drop out of school at present. While only a few years ago, a young boy could easily get at least a few months' work in the woods, especially if he had connections, at present, even seasonal woodswork is difficult to come by.

A new opportunity for employment for both boys and girls lies, as already mentioned, in "going to the mainland." As pointed out in chapter 1, out-migration to the mainland has three significant features: (1) the great majority of migrants are young unmarried people; (2) contrary to common opinion, it is not the *most* educated or the *least* educated who make up the majority of the young migrants, but rather those who drop out of school in grades 9, 10, or 11; (3) the decision to migrate is very much determined by "network" – having close kin or friends who have already migrated. Such connections are crucial economically, in helping to find a job and somewhere to live, as well as socially.

One implication of the third feature is that the migrants tend to cluster first within families and then within neighbourhoods and communities. Hence, some families and communities in Newfoundland lose most of their "crowd" to the mainland, while others may lose none.

A second new opportunity for "employment" is, in fact, furthering one's education. Youth who have dropped out of high school are being offered attractive bursaries or student salaries to go to trade schools or up-grading schools. However, as a twenty year-old boy argued, "It's no good to go to trade school. There's lots of money to it while you're at it, but when you get out you've got nothin' but a trade, no job. Now look at J. J. He took welding. He didn't get a job here and went to Toronto. He tried for a month to get a job there in his trade, but didn't get nothin'. Now he's workin' in a factory, and he's no better off than the fellow with no trade." Others are not this sceptical and put their trust in the government. A man in his early twenties who had up-graded his education said, "If you take the school and get a trade I think the government would look after that you gets a job. Why else would they make people go to school? It would be worse if you go to school and then don't get work. But I wouldn't have gone to school if there had been work."

In fact, many who go to trade schools, training courses, and up-grading schools seem to regard them as a substitute for a job when employment is difficult to find. They do not go to these schools primarily to get training which would qualify them for a particular job, but rather to subsist. As one young man put it: "It's like a job. You gets paid for it don't you? Sometimes I thinks it's more like welfare, though. You don't do nothin', except for yourself." On the other hand, some youth find that they cannot afford to go to school without a drop in their present living standard. One boy of twenty failed grade 9 twice. He then quit school and started to work at a local gas station. His wage was not high ($180 per month), but he was able to keep a good second-hand car by doing most of the repair work himself. He was fairly satisfied with his present situation but saw "no future in it." He wanted to go to an up-grading school for his grade nine and ten, and then to vocational school to study electronics. However, when he applied for the up-grading school, he found that he would not be able to keep his car and that made him drop his plans. "I don't know what to do without me car."

For some young people, both these new opportunities are blocked: they find it difficult to go to the mainland because they have no connections there, and they cannot get into a trade school because they lack experience, or they cannot get into training courses and up-grading school because they did poorly at school and thus feel insecure with regard to formal (academic) training.[3]

The boys who cannot get jobs, who cannot afford cars, and who come from families of low standing in the community because they have been on welfare for a long time, often have difficulty in maintaining friendships with boys who own cars. All these factors stand in the way of their being able to participate in the local youth culture. Such boys are often found "hanging around" and begging rides from anyone. Many whom I had never talked to before came to ask me to drive them to this or that place. This aggressiveness and hanging around reinforce the image of these youth as being "bad boys" from "bad homes" in a "bad neighbourhood" (the Bay).

Their image as bad boys, in turn, makes it difficult for them to obtain employment locally, and the lack of a car complicates the chances of working non-locally. The traditional work available to them in the past was logging and fishing, but the curtailment of logging operations and the lack of devel-

3   As unemployment gets worse and the resulting enrolment increases in the trade schools, up-grading schools and training courses, admission requirements become higher and school performance (grade passed) has become the major criterion for entrance.

opment of the outport fishery have made jobs even in these fields difficult to get. Thus, these boys seem trapped in a vicious circle which is extremely difficult to get out of.

This brings me to the final point I want to discuss in this chapter: the predominance of early marriages in the outports. Most if not all early marriages in Squid Cove seem to be due to pre-marital pregnancies. A basic reason for this is that outport youth have less access to and less knowledge of contraceptives; also both boys and girls are perhaps less careful than middle-class youth in their pre-marital sexual practices. For many girls, an independent career is not something to reckon on; 'career' means primarily marriage and the more so for school drop-outs. As one twenty-year-old boy put it: "When a girl is seventeen around here and not in school, all she thinks about is to get married." Youth of both sexes who, for economic and social reasons, are excluded from participating in the local youth culture seem to be the least careful in sexual matters.

Early marriage and early parenthood in a situation of high unemployment and under-employment are likely to put the new family on welfare. A youth having just himself to take care of is able to make do with only casual employment, while the greater and continuous demands of a family must be met without fail. The only solutions to no employment is to migrate or go on welfare.

Early marriage may act to distinguish the youth with connections and initiative from those without. For some, marriage brings a more stable employment pattern, while for others, it means welfare; prior to marriage, however, both groups are likely to be equally under-employed. The following example illustrates the case in point. A boy and a girl, aged nineteen and seventeen respectively, got married when the girl became pregnant. The boy left for Toronto where he had kin a short time after they married while the girl stayed behind with her parents. Some time after the child was born, the boy came back to take his wife and child to Toronto with him. He had, in the meantime, secured a fairly well-paid job and saved enough money to buy necessary household equipment.

In another case of early marriage following a pregnancy, the young couple stayed with the girl's family and the boy started fishing regularly with his father-in-law who had no sons. After a few years, they became equal partners and the son-in-law made several innovations in their fishing techniques: he got a loan for a new diesel engine, installed a gurdy for hauling nets, and got several new nets so as to double their fishing capacity.

In a third case, the boy secured a job in a construction company through the help of his uncle (his father's brother). This meant that he had to leave his young wife alone for long periods at a time, but she managed to cope because her married sister lived in her husband's community (that is, in the same community).

These examples indicate that an early marriage can have a positive effect in the search for a stable working career; however, all three boys succeeded because one or both newlyweds had helpful kin connections. On the other hand, if work is scarce and neither spouse has connections, an early marriage can easily result in welfare. In one such case, the couple settled near the boy's widowed father who helped them build a small house. The son fished with his father for a living, but after a couple of bad seasons, they found that the fishery could not support them both. The boy was not able to obtain any other regular employment and had to go on welfare for part of the year. In the meantime, the wife gave birth to two more children and, still only nineteen, was incapable of coping with the household duties. The people in the community started to talk about her and her husband. In particular, they were accused of copulating in the middle of the day, and "no wonder she's always pregnant." After some time, the couple moved to the girl's home community where others were on welfare, including the girl's father.

A more drastic case was one where the newly married boy could not get a job at all, and the young couple had to start their marriage on welfare. This seemed to discourage the boy completely and he continued to drink intensively with the friends he had before he married. The couple continued to have children, all the same. The only stability in the marriage was the girl's relationship to her mother-in-law who helped her with the children and mediated between her son and his wife.

With the insecure employment situation in Newfoundland, early marriages and early parenthood certainly increase the extent of welfare and the deprivation that follows. One may feel inclined to suggest that young people should show greater constraint in their sexual practices. On the other hand, to say that these early marriages are the *cause* of much welfare, as many people in Squid Cove and elsewhere do, is only a simplification of the situation. If a cause has to be pinpointed, it would be the lack of employment opportunities. As the cases outlined above indicate, young people are not "unwilling to work" – an indictment of the older working population.

Still, young married men who fail to secure employment and are thus not able themselves to "take care of their families" have the lowest social standing in the outport community. This is not surprising bearing in mind that "honest work" and "good family" rank among the highest values in Newfoundland outports. The situation of these young couples is in complete contrast to George's and Elizabeth's circumstances. In the first place, George has a long working career to look back on which is of intrinsic value to him as well as being of great value in his interpersonal relations, whereas these young men often have no working career to talk about at all.

Secondly, George can excuse himself and is excused by others for being on welfare because he is partly incapacitated; indeed, because he has "worked too hard." On the other hand, even if young men on welfare were incapacitated, they would not likely be excused unless the reason for their disability were absolutely clear, and providing the disability was not due to "youthful carelessness" such as careless driving or speedboating.

Thirdly, it is difficult for a young girl to support the male role of her unemployed husband as Elizabeth is able to do. The young couple have not had the time and the opportunity to build up a relationship of trust and support. In all probability, the young married man would have to turn to his peers to assert his maleness, and being unemployed, this would likely mean other unemployed men. Furthermore, a young married girl will have had less opportunity to establish and maintain a network of personal relations with the other women in her husband's community. Partly because of this, she would be identified more readily with her husband as a "welfare case."

Fourthly, a young man is not able to assert himself through his children's success as George is able to do, because his children have to reach at least school age before they can "prove" themselves. In keeping with this observation, I noticed several young fathers on welfare showing little interest in their children generally, but often favouring the oldest child. They would boast of this child's capabilities for doing the most trivial things, "just like the women," as one man commented.

Fifthly, young men on welfare generally have little "to get their hands at" to keep themselves busy. This is so partly because of the smaller size of their families and of not having a son for a buddy, and also because they have not been able to establish working routines. Moreover, domestic working routines of a traditional kind which involve gardening and fishing, are often regarded as "something only the older people do."

Finally, the young men have not established a network of interpersonal relations to the same extent and of the same content as the older men. Such a network is important not only for its own sake but also for serving as a matrix where the assets outlined above can be played out and given social recognition.

For the young couples having to live on welfare, the scarcity of employment is, in many ways, more critical than for George and other older men, since the possibilities of managing their unemployment within the social and moral confines of a rural community are extremely limited.

"There's Not Much Point in Workin' When Your Neighbour Does Just as Well Doin' Nothin'"

10

This study has focussed on the problems which unemployed welfare recipients experience in attempting to maintain their community status, their self-esteem, and their dignity. Therefore, in this final chapter, instead of summarizing the content of the preceding chapters, I would like to turn to the employed outporters. In concentrating on the unemployed to the extent done in this study, it might not have been possible to always keep in perspective the *employed* men and *their* problems in relation to the welfare recipients.

A discussion of the relationship between employed men and the unemployed welfare recipients has to take as its point of departure the values and meanings attached to work in the outport culture as well as in the society at large. We have seen that work is not valued equally in the outport culture and in the society at large;[1] it may suffice here to summarize how an outport man defines many of his social relationships in terms of his work. It is through his work, in the form of a job or self-employment, that a man earns his living and it is by earning his living that a man claims reciprocity in relation to society and independence in relation to his peers. Work gives a man the position of provider for his family, and work is the major legitimation for the acquisition of material goods. Work, then, puts a man in a complementary position: it gives him a status in relation to the family, the community, the economy, and the polity. All these may be regarded as positive values and meanings of work.

However, working for a living also involves costs or negative values. First, for most men in Squid Cove, work implies that one has to stay away from one's family for long periods of time; second, most types of work open to outport men are labour-oriented and, the outports argue, they will eventually break a man's health down; third, working is not something one generally does for its own sake but rather something one *has* to do. Work,

---

1 Outporters do not evaluate a man according to his occupation to the extent that this is done in an urban industrial culture. Rather, a man is judged according to how 'hard' a worker he is in the occupation at which he works. One may ascribe this peculiar emphasis to the fact that outporters are not occupationally mobile; their evaluation of work is a reflection of the situation of the majority. Also, the notion of a hard worker is not restricted to paid work, but extends to work done for oneself. Indeed, a man who works hard only at his actual job and not for himself may have difficulty in maintaining his reputation as a hard worker.

then, implies a series of costs, and it demands moral strength to take these costs.

Because of its positive value in defining a man's relationships to individuals, groups, and institutions, and because of its costs which demand moral strength, the work role tends towards a kind of moral imperative. Work becomes something one *should* do and something that is morally praiseworthy *because of* the costs involved. Whereas one may be excused from committing oneself to other major roles in the outport culture such as establishing a family, there are few excuses for not working: socially accepted excuses are limited to being too young to work (but preparing for work); being too old to work (but "having done one's lot"); and being too sick to work (but willing to take measures to again become able). That no jobs are available is not generally an excuse for not working if a man is physically capable.[2]

All outporters, employed and unemployed alike, have accepted the 'higher' or overarching value of the welfare state wherein a man and his family should be provided for if he cannot find work; indeed; a man has an obligation to apply for welfare to provide for his family. However, the employed insist on further criteria in order to be able to judge whether an able-bodied man can be excused from working. To be excused a man has to show *willingness* to work and even if it is established that work is not available, this is not taken as sufficient evidence of one's willingness, for *not* being willing to work may be hidden behind an argument that work is not available.

Wanting to work, then, has to be positively proven if a welfare recipient wants to be excused for not working. Hence, a major part of the management of unemployment is consequently concerned with communicating one's desire for work. The main ways to do so is by stressing one's past working career (see Ch. 2), by looking for work (see Ch. 3), and by working for oneself (see Ch. 6).

For the present theme, it is most significant that the employed men in Squid Cove are often critical and dispute the claims put forward by the unemployed. Several examples of such mistrust have been given throughout this study. Even a long working career can be negated as evidence of a welfare recipient's willingness to work, and statements such as the following are common: "Well, but he was never a *hard* worker"; or "Well, he's not

2   It should be noted that housewives are excused from taking a job even if their husbands are unemployed. Also, it is legitimate for unmarried girls to stay home and help their mothers after they have left school (cf. Ch. 5 and 9). Allowances for unmarried mothers are also made, the critical point being whether the mother takes good care of her child(ren). Granted, few jobs are available to outport women, but cultural factors – the image of what a woman and a man should be – are the decisive factors in excusing persons from taking a job.

working that much *now*, is he?" One should note the subtle way these statements are phrased if the aim is to bring the unemployed men's claims into disrepute. The first statement is difficult to check without a detailed knowledge of the whole working career of the man in question while the second is likely, for audiences without such knowledge, to draw attention to how "hard" and how much the unemployed man is *presently* working and at what kind of work. Subsistence production combined with maintenance of house may not provide enough hours to make a working-day out of every day, not least of "hard" work (see Ch. 6). But even if an unemployed man were successful in occupying himself in hard work, he would likely be criticized for just that because he has the whole day to work for himself while the employed man has only his spare time. Hence, the welfare recipient is caught in a dilemma and to be free of any criticism whatever, he must strike a balance between not working too hard, but hard enough.

Another common way to refuse the unemployed welfare recipient full moral status is to question the premise for his having to go on welfare at all; that is, the non-availability of work. The fact that there is no work is often disputed by the employed, and their argument is plausible since the exact state of the labour market is difficult to assess. Also, the state of the labour market changes, often radically, over time. This is especially the case with the Newfoundland labour market because of the seasonality of the primary industries and because construction is a major industry; it is "a job just to get a job." Thus, one often hears workers, especially construction workers argue that the unemployed recipients "show lack of initiative" and "don't even look for a job."

It should be noted that in such statements, the basic question of whether work is available takes a secondary place while attention is focussed instead on the behaviour of the unemployed — which is possible to observe. The implication is that the argument is reduced from a structural macro-level — the state of the labour market — to an individual micro-level — the individual act of looking for work.

We find, then, three common elements in the argument used by the employed against the unemployed: it is highly personalized in the sense that it can be directly related to the individual and his moral status; (2) it is highly standardized and in the form of a series of phrases which most people know; and (3) taken together, the criticisms form a syndrome in which there is a counter-phrase for every excuse the unemployed may have.

Another complaint of most employed men, especially of those with lower incomes, is that the 'income' received by welfare recipients is comparable to what one earns by working. "There'll soon be no difference between what a man gets on welfare and what a man gets from working"; or "there's not much point in workin' when your neighbour can get as much stayin' home doin' nothin'." When an employed man makes these statements, he is not criticizing or disputing the value of working for a living, but rather the welfare recipients' receiving and the welfare authorities' giving out such large amounts. Perhaps, also, he is protesting his own low wages. On the other hand, if a welfare recipient made the same remarks, it could hardly be interpreted otherwise than the fact that he is disputing the value of work. Furthermore, it would be interpreted as an indictment against the outport worker for working (hard) in spite of low wages, and therefore, for being rather foolish for not going on welfare instead.

In a similar vein, the employed also complain that welfare demands no obligation to reciprocate goods. A statement often heard is that welfare recipients "don't do nothin' for the money they get." In fact, this is the feeling of many welfare recipients (cf. George's appeal in Ch. 3: "Why can't the government let me work for the money they now give me?"). This complaint is the basis for the claim made by most employed men that "by goin' to the government, a man loses his independence."

In this connection, it should be noted that the decisions which allow a man to go on welfare and the amount he is paid are outside the control of the local community; these decisions belong to the welfare authorities. In effect, then, when the employed man makes the statements mentioned above, he is criticizing the welfare regulations and the authorities responsible for them.[3] However, the welfare recipients are censured at the same time.

The arguments outlined above may be seen as an effort by the employed to communicate and underline the basic qualities which they see as comprising the *moral community* of Squid Cove. Squid Cove, they claim, is a community where a man's moral worth is measured by his ability and willingness to work. If we step back and examine the situation analytically, it is probable that Squid Cove and other outport communities with a substantial number of unemployed[4] are experiencing a split in their moral community.

Behind this conflict, there lies a basic dilemma for both the unemployed

3 It should be noted that the ideology of the welfare state as regards able-bodied relief is corrupted by the employed in that the intentions behind the rules and regulations of welfare are transformed and reevaluated as they are incorporated into the culture and social structure of the local community. One may go further in this line of reasoning and argue that the rules and regulations put down by a central bureaucracy can seldom, not to say never, take account of, or take precautions against these corruptions when the rules are applied locally. Bureaucratic rules will seldom or never fit the system of values and the social structure of a local community.

4 A question which would be of great theoretical interest and also for social policy-making is one of ratio: is there a relationship between the way unemployed welfare recipients are treated, and the number of recipients compared with the number of employed men residing in the community? More specifically, is a community's or neighbourhood's capacity to incorporate welfare recipients in its moral community limited by personal networks and the process of ghettorization? Is ghettorization partly to be explained by an overspill of welfare recipients?

and employed. For the employed, the increase in the number of welfare recipients is felt to constitute a threat to the value of work and thus to their self-image; for many unemployed, their 'aggressive' arguing is an effort to maintain their dignity. Furthermore, the behaviour of the welfare recipients not only constitutes a threat to the moral community as expounded by the employed, but also infers that many unemployed form their own moral community, but then in a negative sense. This seems to be one basis for the tendency to impute a wide range of imperfections to the Bay people on the basis of the original one: unemployment. We have seen that some of these imputed imperfections are false (Ch. 8), while others are true. But then they are not viewed as imperfections by the Bay people: "sticking together", for instance, is regarded by them as neighbourliness, talking "straight" as being honest, and insisting on their "rights" as a duty towards their families.

Furthermore, there are those among the unemployed (in particular, the Bay people in Squid Cove) who state outright that they consider welfare a right and not in any sense a privilege, and that welfare payments are not much to live on. Many of the Bay men also stated their unwillingness to take jobs that paid less than what they were able to get on welfare. Some argued that the government had a duty to create jobs locally and refused to take jobs outside the region if they were not relatively well-paid and permanent. On the whole, they appeared to be rather calculating about working compared with being on welfare and thus explicitly questioned the moral imperative to work.

On the other hand, most employed men in Squid Cove, together with many unemployed consider such statements to be self-righteous, demanding, aggressive, and "showing no shame." They also insist that the Bay people *develop* such arguments to defend their unwillingness to work. In this way, the employed legitimize avoiding interaction with the unemployed, or at least, avoid considering the validity of their "rights."

All in all, the conflicts result in a lowering of the *collective* standard of living of the community. Unemployment affects not only those who become unemployed but it also makes community life unpleasant and problematic for those who still work. Men who were previously workmates and/or friends find they cannot talk to each other the way they used to do; former workmates begin avoiding each other; many men find they can no longer take part in public interaction and use public spaces; and aggressive arguments and 'double-talk' increase. All these changes are relevant to the concept, standard of living, although they are not included in the ways standard of living is currently measured in the welfare state.

Any economic system harbouring imperfections which necessitate large-scale welfare policies such as able-bodied relief will constantly be in danger of reflecting premises to communities that cause a split in the moral community and thus a reduction of the collective standard of living. Herein lies the paradox of the welfare state: its services are in many ways 'anti-services' to communities. Providing economic security to men (and their families) who fail to secure employment is a rather easy administrative matter and something which most modern industrial states can afford. But economic security provided through welfare sparks off new forms of *social* deprivation that derive from unemployment, and there seems to be no solutions to these social problems within the present framework of the welfare state.

No welfare state so far has found itself in a position to guarantee work for everybody. In George's words, "I guess it's cheaper for the government to keep a fellow on welfare than to give him work." Although neither the unemployed nor I (having concentrated my attention on the problems of unemployment on the micro-level) am able to substantiate such a claim, the mere existence of high rates of unemployment suggests that it might indeed be "cheaper for the government." The welfare state, then, may be said to convert economic and political costs to social costs. Furthermore, it allows these social costs to be carried by the unemployed person himself, his family, and his community.

Appendix: The Field Work

The anthropologist refers to his main method of gathering data as field work. In the most general sense, field work involves living in the midst of the particular people one is studying for a long period of time, ideally a year or more. In this way, the anthropologist tries "to immerse himself in a way of life that is not his own" (Hannerz, 1969:201); he tries to participate as much as possible in the doings of the people he is studying. One might say that the anthropologist tries 'to go native' both behaviourally through participant observation and also emotionally (but not cognitively, because then he would no longer be able to do anthropology).

Only by participant observation, the anthropologist believes, can one get an understanding of how and why people behave the way they do. This understanding is largely arrived at by observing people in their natural physical and social settings. Other means of collecting data made use of by the field worker are (more or less) the structured interview and the gathering of statistical facts. The latter are reliable methods for getting particular types of information, but for most of the data the social scientist is interested in, formal questioning is insufficient since it involves introducing a particular context and most often, not a natural one. Through participant observation, the field worker himself becomes part of the context within which the people he is studying act, and he, therefore, may unduly influence their behaviour and thus destroy the naturalness of the situation. The field worker is acutely aware of this and, while he cannot help being a part of the entity he is studying, he uses every means possible to be 'a fly on the wall.' His prolonged stay in the field is one way of making people used to seeing him, and in many realms of behaviour, it is too inconvenient for people to constantly take account of the anthropologist in order not to "do things the way they are used to."

However, sometimes the anthropologist's presence often does influence the context, and there are many situations where he is not allowed to participate or where it is not appropriate that he be present. The most the field worker can do about this is to try to be accepted by the people he is studying on their own terms. If he is interested in studying close social relations, he has to become a link in his informants' chain of personal relations: a friend, a co-resident, a neighbour, or in many small-scale societies, an adopted kinsman (cf. Briggs, 1970).

In other words, the field worker has to have a recognized role or roles to be able to interact, and hence participate with the people he wants to study. Normally, the role or roles which the field worker ends up with are the result of a joint effort by his informants and himself. Sometimes, though, the field worker is *given* a role by the people he is studying and there is often little he can do about this (see Briggs, *op. cit.*); at other times, the field worker can *take* a role, say that of district officer (Axel Sommerfelt, personal communication). While in the latter case, the role has to be known to the informants to be effective, in the former case the role need not be known to the field worker.

The roles which the field worker ends up with are of crucial importance to his participation in the society and thus to what he is able to observe of it; and the roles he acquires are generally less determined by the personality of the field worker than by the culture of the society he is working in. Also, it should be noted that some roles are often mutually exclusive in the sense that, being a kinsman, friend, or neighbour to some informants implies *not* being so to others. Many field workers (including the author) have been caught up in networks of personal relations (roles) from which it was diffi-cult to become disentangled.

There are further problems. Even if the field worker is successful in establishing an optimal set of roles, he will have difficulties in being com-pletely committed to them because he has to record his observations while he participates (Briggs, *op. cit.*). Also, in his efforts to record a variety of facts about particular people as well as the culture, he may find that much of the data he pursues is inappropriate for someone in his assumed native role to record or even to know (*op. cit.*).

Of course, the field worker never wholly succeeds in participating in everything that goes on in the society he is studying, nor is he ever able to perform adequately in existing roles. He will always be a stranger to some extent – an outsider. On the other hand, the research of a large number of anthropologists and sociologists indicates that the analysis of the field worker seems "closer to life" than that gathered by any other method. One basic reason for this is that it is more convenient for people, having to cope with a field worker's intrusion, to give him a role with which they are familiar than to keep him outside their realm of relationships.

* * *

What has been said so far may be taken as a short list of problems regard-ing field work and field workers in general. Every field worker has, of course, his own specific problems depending on, among other things, his research interests, his theoretical and methodological orientation, the time at his disposal, his personal background and personality, and (assuredly), the society in which he is working. In my own case, I decided to investigate

how individuals and families adapt to and manage long-term unemployment
and living off public welfare in small rural (outport) communities.

My interest in unemployment and welfare arose from field work in a
number of Newfoundland outports the previous year. During this time, I
was researching the socio-economic changes in Newfoundland since it became the tenth province of Canada, and particularly the effects political
decisions on the macro-level had on the adaptation of the many small outport
fishing and logging communities. One of the major government (federal, as
well as provincial) policies regarding a large number of these outports was
to encourage people, not least financially, to move to larger centres. The
main factors behind this policy were (i) that the outporters' demands for
public services such as schools, hospitals, roads, wharfs, and others were
too expensive for the government to install in every small community, and
(ii) that the outports had too meagre a resource base to provide a fair living
standard; alternatively, greater opportunities for earning a living would be
available in the larger centres since the province was encouraging the establishment of modern industries in them.

After investigating the effects of the government policies in a number of
outports in northeastern Newfoundland, I came to the conclusion that, on the
whole, the so-called resettlement programme provided neither better public
services nor greater opportunities for employment. Rather, I argued (Wadel,
1968) for a selective redevelopment programme in outport fishing communities simultaneously with an industrialization programme in the larger centres.
I based my argument on two factors: (1) that many outports have a greater
potential for development than had been thought, especially if a province-
wide marketing organization were established to enable fishermen to sell
all their catches and get a fair price for their product (see Brox, 1972);
(2) the increasing amount of unemployment and under-employment in
the province would not be solved through resettlement; on the contrary,
resettlement increased unemployment (cf. Iverson and Matthews, 1967).
A better solution, I suggested, would be government-initiated programmes
for maintaining and improving already existing livelihoods (Wadel, *op. cit.*).

From this focus on the opportunities for employment in traditional outport adaptations, I developed my interest in people who depended mainly
or solely on welfare for a living.

During this early field work, I did not try to investigate in great depth the
social and economic situation of the welfare recipients, the ones unemployed
more or less all year round. But of course I recognized that the problems
of these people were particularly acute and I became interested in how they
managed to maintain their self-respect and their social relations within the
small outport communities. When I inquired into the matter, however, I
found it a very delicate field of investigation. Both the welfare recipients
I met, and their neighbours, kin, and friends seemed extremely reluctant

to talk about their situations. Furthermore, opportunities for direct observation of how the recipients and the better-situated managed relations between themselves were limited. While most outporters found it quite acceptable for me to go fishing, logging, and engage in various subsistence activities with them, "staying around the house" with a welfare recipient for a longer period of time was found to be odd and inappropriate. During one period when I interacted extensively with a young welfare recipient for several days in a row, some of my neighbours even came and told me that this young man "was bad company, in case you didn't know."

In preparing to write up my data and reading through my field notes several times, I became aware of my incomplete understanding of the situation of the unemployed.

I have to admit that while in the field, I came to share (to some extent) some of my "good neighbours' " negative views of the aforementioned young man as well as other welfare recipients. I found some of them somewhat aggressive, as did my neighbours. The young man, for instance, would come and ask me to drive him to neighbouring communities, to go fishing, and to show me this and that place. After some time, I felt he tried to keep me to himself, and to prevent me from interacting with other people. (Before I took steps to extricate myself from this relationship, however, he solved my problem by moving to his wife's home community where I visited him several times.)

Besides my tendency to adopt a negative view of welfare recipients, they were marginal to my main interest of outport redevelopment. Any development, I believed, had to start with the model provided by the better-adapted, and the welfare recipients would then be able to advance themselves through a general development of the outport economy. These attitudes of mine were reinforced through many conversations I had with outport leaders and entrepreneurs as well as with Newfoundland politicians and some of my colleagues interested in outport development.

It was only in the final phase of writing up my analysis that I had second thoughts, and began to believe that the outport welfare recipients were likely to be excluded from a development process. At least, they would be the last to profit from any kind of outport development. In going through my notes, I could see that there were processes which tended to belittle not only individual welfare recipients, but also families and neighbourhoods and even whole communities. In my notes, I had used the term "welfare community" several times. To a large extent, the communities or settlements I had thus named were those where inshore fishing was not the major livelihood but rather communities situated in bays and further inland where access to the fishing grounds was poor. Traditionally, the population in these "bay" communities had taken their main livelihood from the forest as loggers for the paper companies or in small-scale saw mills. Fishing, especially lobster fishing, was often a subsidiary occupation. With the mechanization of the logging

industry drastically reducing the demand for labour, and with the closing
down of many of the saw mills (partly due to the Canadian mainland competition), these communities experienced more unemployment than the fishing
communities. Moreover, unemployment and thus welfare dependency
tended to be year-round. With these thoughts, I decided to carry out my
next field work in a "bay" outport as well as a fishing outport, and focus my
research on the situation of the unemployed welfare recipients in a community context.

* * *

I rented a house for myself and my family (wife and three children) in a
"bay" community I have called Squid Cove where much of the population
was unemployed. This community was also conveniently located in relation
to three neighbouring communities only a few miles away where I planned
to do field work simultaneously with that in Squid Cove. The four communities differed in the extent of welfare that prevailed as well as in other respects:
in two, fishing was the major occupation and in the third, both fishing and
logging were carried out. They also differed in size, in religious affiliation,
and in social history. By studying several communities, I hoped to be better
able to isolate the effects of various factors on the situation of the unemployed welfare recipient.

I started field work by spending some time in each community. My two
field assistants took censuses of two of the communities and I did the same
in Squid Cove. (I had taken a census of one community the previous
year.) In the first few weeks, I also tried to investigate the activity cycles
of the various communities. In the fishing villages, I went fishing with
various crews and from my conversations with them, I was able to plot the
yearly cycles. I made one short trip to a logging camp further inland to get
to know the logging routines. I also participated in the various subsistence
activities such as hunting, fishing, woodcutting, and gardening, and in the
various social occasions in the churches, the shops, the dance halls, besides
interacting as much as I could on the roads, the wharves and in the homes of
people.

Having had five months of field work in the same general area the previous year, I had no difficulties in getting into contact with people. I had
participated in a couple of Fishermen's Radio Broadcasts the previous winter
and a number of the fishermen and others had heard me. The fact that I was
from Norway and had studied fishing communities in that country, made it
possible to make conversation on a 'give-and-take' basis; a remark on my
part about Norway acted as a cue to inquire about what things were like in
Newfoundland. My initial role then, was that of a Norwegian - teaching - at -
the - University - who - wants - to - know - about - Newfoundland - and -
maybe - write - a - book - about - the - outports.

Also, the fact that I had visited most of the settlements in the area previously and had acquired a general knowledge of them, made it possible for me to use this knowledge in a give-and-take way. Hence, conversations with both men and women in Squid Cove and the neighbouring communities often began with statements (by me) such as "I talked to a' man (woman) over in X Cove and he told me that ...", to which the local people would reply with a statement about Squid Cove.

Another factor which facilitated interaction was that I often met people who had kin, friends, or acquaintances in the other communities I had been to. In cases where I was able to establish common acquaintanceship in this way, the conversation could at once be more personal. On several occasions, when my somewhat direct questioning caused reluctance to answer, establishing a common acquaintance generally broke the ice and ensured a more positive response. Besides my status as a Norwegian/teacher/writer, then, I was often able to pose as a kind of quasi-acquaintance, and this allowed me to inquire about the things which were of the greatest interest to me, namely personal opinions and attitudes in the community.

After becoming acquainted with several local people in this way, it was easier to enter into conversations with other people in the community. I would also use the census data on kinship relations and on careers to further conversation. Sometimes, when a name was mentioned, I could say, "That's your brother-in-law, isn't it?" This remark might then encourage the man to whom I was talking to make a few remarks about the brother-in-law. Such information picked up in passing often could not have been obtained by direct questioning; it also gave clues to social relations between people. In conversations with several men simultaneously, my questions as to places and individuals figuring in a story, what may be called background or context information, also often led to prolonged discussions between the men themselves; I became a mere supernumerary which, of course, is the ideal position for a field worker.

Besides my concern with being able to observe people behaving as naturally as possible, I too, had to appear to behave as natural as possible from the informants' point of view. That meant, first of all, *not* asking too many questions, in too direct a manner. It also meant that I had to relate my conversations to the kind of relationship I had been able to establish with a particular individual at a particular time. Information thus came in bits and pieces, the importance of which I was often not able to evaluate at the time it was given. Most of it went into my note books as raw data; that is, "A said ... I said ... B said ... A said," and so on.

I did not state my special interest in the situation of unemployed welfare recipients (except to people I came to know fairly well), but inquired into it under a general interest in the outports. Early in the field work, whenever I followed up a conversation which had to do specifically with people on welfare, the response was slow and non-specific, and someone would change the subject. People seemed to understand and accept my interest in fishing, logging, and subsistence activities, but not in unemployment and welfare. At least, this was usually the case when there were several people together. In a dyad, and within a family setting, I could bring up the topic of welfare and get strong views even about particular individuals and families.

During the first months, I had some success in establishing contact with men and families relying largely on public assistance for their living and some couples whom I visited talked rather frankly about their situations. From such conversations, I came to understand the various defences and sources of self-esteem the different families made use of. What I was not able to do, was to observe these families interacting with their neighbours and friends. Or rather, my own presence seemed to influence unduly their behaviour, largely, it seems, because I was included as a member of their group and thus acted as a kind of buffer in their interaction with others.

Let me illustrate. I came to know a man who lived largely off public welfare through one of my field-assistants who had boarded with him during his census-taking. On most occasions when we got together with other people, he would say, "Come now, let's go into the house and talk." Inside, both he and his wife would talk freely about their situation, economic as well as social. He would also talk about all his friends and kin in the community, but he would never take me to see them. When we sat together with other men in the shop, on the wharf, or were just walking along the road, he generally tried to lead the conversation and tell the others about me or what I had told him earlier, for example, about Norway. He seldom involved me in his conversations with the other men. Thus, he seemed to try to make me his own special "friend." He managed this to the extent that in my interaction with his neighbours and co-residents without his presence, they were reluctant to make anything but general remarks about him. Sensing their reluctance, I found it impossible to ask questions, not even indirectly. I felt sure that the other men understood how this man used me, but they feigned ignorance and said nothing. From their behaviour, I deduced that the man was more isolated and had fewer "friends" in the community than he would admit to me, but I never got to know the basis for this. Together with other experiences of a similar nature, it made me realize that I would have great difficulty in becoming incorporated into the *network* of personal relations of a welfare recipient by being a daily visitor to a community. At this stage, George became crucial to my field work situation.

* * *

On my second day in Squid Cove, I met my next-door neighbour whom I have called George. The house we rented belonged to George's daughter and son-in-law, and so at first our relationship was one of house-agent and tenants as George and Elizabeth were looking after the house in their absence. My wife and I had no knowledge of George's situation when we approached them about renting the house; we had driven by the house and had seen that nobody was living there then.

At the time, George had a job making improvements at the local provincial park, but was laid off a week or so after we arrived. Then he spent more time around the house and we got to talk more. From the start, George talked extensively about the scarcity of work locally as well as in the province in general. On my eleventh day in Squid Cove, I recorded the following statement by George: "I was laid off (from the park) on Friday, but there's lots of work to do there still. I think the government has used all the money they have for that. Now, what's wrong? I'm willin' to work but there's no work around. Now, whose fault is that? There's hundreds of men like me in Newfoundland."

George also talked a lot about his working career; that he had worked twenty-seven seasons as a logger, that he had hurt his back some years ago and was not able to engage in heavy work any longer, that he was not sick enough to qualify for a medical certificate because he could still do light work and, indeed, felt himself competent to do light work, that he was now fifty-four years old and still had seven children at school.

George's remarks about all these matters were, by and large, uttered in a rather casual manner, and were interjected with practical comments about what we were doing, when he was helping me with some repairs on the house, for example. Some remarks were uttered while we were alone and others while we were together with Elizabeth, some of their children and/or some of our other neighbours. With regard to the latter situations, I later understood that George was not just talking to me, but as much to the neighbours present. I also learned that the others had heard George's stories several times before, but the fact that I was a stranger and did not know them allowed him to remark on his situation more directly.

Although later I realized that George had been one of my best informants from the very beginning of the field work, my relationship to him was initially not only, and in my own consciousness, not even primarily that of field worker to informant. In the course of having to look after the needs of our family (we had no running water, only a wooden stove for heating as well as for cooking, very little furniture in the house, and inappropriate clothing for the children and ourselves), my wife and I had to ask our neighbours for advice and help for a number of things. My wife found herself turning to Elizabeth, and I to George, for most of it. My wife and I were not in a position to reciprocate as fully as we would have liked to nor sufficiently to meet George's and Elizabeth's standards. Our services consisted largely in driving them to neighbouring communities and towns for shopping, visiting kin, and other purposes.

Our lack of opportunity to score full reciprocity was seemingly appreciated by George, and we came to be in kind of a debt-relation to him. When I occasionally offered to pay him for supplying me with firewood or for doing some "carpenter work" in the house, he would not accept. At the same time, I soon became aware that the few services my wife and I did were important to him for their symbolic value of showing himself and his co-residents that we accepted him. Later I learned that this asymmetrical exchange was typical of George's relations with many of his (other) neighbours, also (cf. Ch. 7).

In our exchanges, both George and Elizabeth and my wife and I tended to overvalue each other's prestations: we undercommunicated the value of our own prestations ("Oh, that was nothing ...") and overcommunicated the value of the prestation we received ("It was very good of you. I don't know how I would have managed without you ..."). For my wife and myself, this came naturally as we would have had great difficulty in managing a number of things on our own, in particular the chores that had to be done to maintain the household.

The various types of services rendered us by George and his family and the over-evaluation are based on the outport custom of neighbourliness. Neighbourliness also involved socializing and visiting, and because George was around the house most of the time, I saw him almost every day. My wife visited and was visited by Elizabeth every day, often several times a day. Also, our three children found their best friends among George's and Elizabeth's children. The point to be noted here is that in interacting so extensively, we did only what was customary in a Newfoundland outport; close neighbours are supposed to interact daily and in a friendly manner. Not to do so would be looked upon as odd, if not offensive. To us, then, George was initially as much a neighbour as an informant, and I had to act as much as a neighbour as a field worker. Moreover, whenever the roles of neighbour and field worker came into conflict, as they often did, the role of neighbour had to take precedence because I had to look after my family, first and foremost.

All in all, we interacted more with George and his family than with our other neighbours. This could have resulted in negative feelings on their part towards both George and us – in George's case, for trying to make us his 'property.' However, this did not happen since my wife and I insisted on socializing with all our neighbours and George could not – even if he wanted to – control our relationships. Also, being our house-agent, George had an acceptable reason for interacting more with us than with the other neighbours.

My social relations and roles, and consequently my field work situation were thus very different within the neighbourhood in which I resided from those in other neighbourhoods in Squid Cove and particularly in other communities where I was just a visitor. While in the latter situations, I was conscious of my role as field worker first and foremost, within my own neighbourhood I had to be conscious of my roles as head of a family and as neighbour, as much as field worker. Although my neighbours certainly considered my family and myself as outsiders and strangers and as visitors to the neighbourhood and community, in many day-to-day routines they would treat us as their neighbours.

This incorporation into the neighbourhood was, as already mentioned, based on the outport custom of neighbourliness The point that I would like to stress here, however, is that the style of behaviour outport neighbours have among themselves would have made it somewhat awkward for my neighbours *not* to treat us as neighbours in many contexts. For had they not chosen to treat us as neighbours, they would have had to co-ordinate, synchronize, and possibly change their style of behaviour, and this would have been inconvenient over a period of six months. Thus, our neighbours were motivated not only by kindness (as my wife and I often looked at it), but also by the most convenient route open to them. To give us the status of neighbour seemed to be the best way to deal with our intrusion into their neighbourhood.

To be incorporated into the neighbourhood in this sense was not only convenient to my wife and myself as householders, but also to myself as a field worker. It meant that my neighbour would behave "naturally," or as they were used to in most, if not all, contexts. In our neighbourhood, people did not treat me as a visitor to the same extent as they did when I visited other neighbourhoods and communities: my wife and I became part of the network of social relations within the neighbourhood to some degree. Although we could still influence the behaviour of our neighbours, the fact that they had decided to treat us as neighbours made it possible for us to isolate our influence; that is, to see when and where we got special treatment and when our neighbours were being influenced by our presence while interacting among themselves.

I might give an instance where I found my presence did influence behaviour. It was noted earlier that when George talked to me in the presence of some of his other neighbours about his own situation, his long working career, and his incapacity to do heavy work, he seemed to be directing his talk to them, reminding them whose fault it was that he was on welfare. My presence, then, made it possible for him to make remarks about his situation more directly and to the point than it would have been possible if he had talked only to his neighbours. Furthermore, in the course of such conversations he would often ask for support: "Now, isn't that so Peter?" and Peter, more likely than not, replied in the affirmative. However, the reply seemed to imply more than just the affirmation of a fact; his neighbour affirmed that George certainly could be excused for being on welfare. What is more, George managed, by my presence, to get his neighbour to make such a supportive statement publicly, in the presence of others. Hence, it was more binding: the neighbour would find it difficult to deny such statements later, especially if he were not completely sure that the other neighbour(s) was of the same opinion.

The other neighbours were, of course, in the same situation in relation to my wife and myself: they could not be sure of our opinion of George and so they would hesitate about conveying any negative opinions they might have of him. The fact that my wife and I socialized extensively with George and his family would also be interpreted as a sign that we had a high opinion of George (which we had) and their criticism of George, if any, would be suppressed in our presence. In this way, I might not have got a true picture of George's neighbours' appreciation of him; it might have been more negative than I was given to understand.

Although I have to admit that there is a possibility of this being the case, I do not believe it was so for several reasons. First, I became aware of the possibility early in the field work and tried to register any hint of negative feelings in the behaviour of George's neighbours and friends. Secondly, and related to the first point, I had six months to find out, and it would have been difficult to hide and pretend for such a length of time. Thirdly, and most importantly, by residing in the middle of the neighbourhood, I had ample opportunity to observe George's frequent interaction with his neighbours (and other people who came to his house). I was also able to visit people in our neighbourhood without George and Elizabeth being present.

The effect of this and other similar 'discoveries' with regard to my field work was an increased consciousness of the difficulties of getting to know how people *really* felt towards welfare recipients. To 'get at' this knowledge required a different type of field work than I had hitherto practised. After a month or so, I therefore decided to postpone my original plan to study several communities simultaneously, and instead concentrate on understanding George's situation in greater depth. Although I continued to visit the other communities, I used these trips largely to check on various aspects of the welfare recipient's situation I had discovered through participant observation in Squid Cove, and particularly in the neighbourhood I resided.

My main concern from this time on was to try to plot and grasp the content of George's total network of interpersonal relations together with the corresponding activities he engaged in. As regards the latter, I went fishing, hunting, and wood-cutting with George, all activities providing opportunities to observe George interacting with other men, often people whom he was marginally acquainted with or who were complete strangers to him. Accompanying us on these trips often was a friend or neighbour or George's own boys. Hence, the trips allowed me to observe George relating to a wide range of people, from his closest kin to strangers, and to observe him do this in the presence of various categories of people.

Besides, my field strategy became one of being an integral part of George's network of personal relations, and to a certain extent, I feel that I succeeded. First, my status as his next-door neighbour extended beyond the boundaries of our neighbourhood to interaction with people outside it, as well. Secondly, George talked about me as his friend and some of his friends, in turn (often, also his kin), began to refer to me as a friend. Lastly, the fact that I concentrated my attention on Squid Cove and particularly on George's neighbourhood, made it possible for me to undercommunicate my role as field worker; instead of having to question directly, I was able to get the data I wanted by just living in the community. This state of affairs also made it easier for people to regard me as just a friend, neighbour, or visiting co-resident.

Of course, at the same time, this strategy limited the number of people I came into contact with. I could not socialize as much as I wanted to within the other neighbourhoods in Squid Cove. To some extent, this was compensated by my interacting in George's network which extended to these other neighbourhoods. I thus got into the Bay neighbourhood through George's former workmate and friend, John (cf. Ch. 8). It should be added that I interacted with many Bay people individually, but then, under the constraints already mentioned above – as a visitor.

As a result of the change in my field work strategy, my relationship with George gradually became more personal, and I felt that I had to state the purpose of my stay more clearly. At first, I had told him that I was a teacher at Memorial University and that I was interested in how people lived in Newfoundland, particularly in the small rural communities; also that I planned to write a book about my impressions. These reasons seemed to satisfy George, particularly since I came from a foreign country and also because of the difficulties the small communities in Newfoundland experienced at the time. Indeed, George, as well as many other outporters often told me that "someone ought to write about all the problems we have to face in the outports."

On the other hand, I did not disclose my special interest in the situation of welfare recipients because I thought people would find it inappropriate. Not until I decided to make George's situation a focus of my research did I tell him about my interest in the situation of the unemployed and that I wanted to write a book on what it was like to be on welfare, using his statements in the book. George accepted this, as long as I did not mention his name. I do not think, however, that he understood how anthropologists write; if he had, perhaps he would not have approved the present exposition. I should add that I had not planned to write the book in this way.

The fact that I told George about the real purpose of my stay in Squid Cove did not change his behaviour towards me or any of his neighbours, as far as I was able to tell. To him, it seemed to be a minor point in our relationship, the basic reason for this being that, in so many ways, we had come to behave as one neighbour to another and as one householder to another. The fact that I was a field worker and he my informant at the same time, could not take precedence.

My relative status to George varied according to the situation. Most of the time, I think I was a stranger standing outside his own status system, but being sympathetic to his situation. For example, he might classify me along with the high school teachers, as a man with learning, and thus as a person with a higher status than himself. Other times, as happened when he was helping me with something around the house, or when we were fishing, hunting, or woodcutting, he seemed to regard me as a junior partner or even as a novice or young boy.

In other situations, George treated me as a confidant, as a man who understood his situation and with whom he could talk openly. Then, I felt George regarded me as a close friend, that ours was a relationship where status was irrelevant.

* * *

We left Squid Cove at the end of December, 1968, as I had to return to my teaching obligations at Memorial University. At that time, I changed my plans of writing a study of unemployment in several communities with different ecological, demographic, and socio-historical backgrounds. Instead, I decided to focus the study on a limited number of cases or histories of unemployed men with different backgrounds: an unemployed middle-aged logger (George), an unemployed fisherman in the same age group, and a younger man with a background in each of these occupations. At one stage, I also planned to include some cases from an urban setting in an effort to isolate the major differences between urban and rural unemployment. The emphasis, in all cases, was to be on the network of personal relations which the various unemployed were able to maintain, and which I had found to be crucial in upholding one's social status within the community. Such a study, I realized, would involve doing field work in several communities, separately, necessitating at least another year.

As it turned out, I was unable to carry out further field work because of other commitments, except for one month in Squid Cove during the summer of 1969. However, as a result of several discussions I had with my colleagues at Memorial and with my wife, in particular, I was encouraged to write up my data on the problems of being on welfare in a rural community, with George and his family as the central characters.

The reasoning behind the approach has already been outlined in the *Introduction* and need not be repeated. At this point, I want to add one further remark concerning scientific anthropological research and personal social commitment.

Most anthropology studies are read by a limited number of people, largely by other anthropologists and sociologists. This is partly due to factors outside the anthropologist's control, but it is also due to the way the anthropologist presents his findings. To reach a larger audience, one would have to write in a way which could be understood and appreciated by the non-specialist. One means which has proven advantageous to this end is a 'personalization' of the presentation. Many of the studies by Oscar Lewis have reached far beyond the world of anthropologists because of such an approach. However, only a small proportion of the themes an anthropologist takes up for study allows for such an approach; among these themes are poverty and deprivation.

The author's mode of presentation reflects, of course, what he *wants* with his study, and here there are many different views: some purely scientific, others purely political, most perhaps a mixture of the two and ideally, without the one contradicting the other. My intentions in this study were to try to combine the two views, hopefully without contradiction. Certainly, I want the reader to gain a further understanding of what it is to be an unemployed welfare recipient in a rural setting. But at the same time, I also want the study to have some influence in changing the negative attitude which seems to prevail in western societies towards people on welfare, and which prevailed in Squid Cove. To a large extent, the attitudes at the local level is a reflection of those held by society in general, and only a change at the macro-level could change the attitude at the micro-level. Moreover, the extent of unemployment is outside the control of the local communities, and nothing short of a *political* decision at the state level could put an end to large-scale unemployment. This, of course, requires an active employment policy. That it can be carried out, even without increasing the rate of inflation more than is 'normal,' has been shown by the Scandinavian countries, for instance.

From what has been said so far, it should be clear that I am not much in doubt about "whose fault it is." It is *not* the fault of the unemployed individual. If this study were summarized into a simple and clear statement, it would be that it is unemployment itself which produces behaviour on the part of the unemployed which makes people blame the unemployment on the individual, and *not* the other way around: that a special attitude or personal defect produces unemployment, as many people – including many Squid Cove inhabitants – seem to think. However, the processes which produce the behaviour which again puts the blame on the individual are complex and not generally clear to the people concerned. It is my hope that this study has been able to uncover some of these processes.

References

BAKKE, E. WIGHT
1940 *Citizens without Work*. New Haven, Yale University Press.

BARBER, BERNARD
1961 "Family Status, Local-Community Status, and Social Stratification: Three Types of Social Ranking." *Pacific Sociological Review*, IV(1).

BARNES, J. A.
1954 "Class and Committees in a Norwegian Island Parish." *Human Relations*, VII(1).

BARTH, FREDRIK (ed.)
1969 *Ethnic Groups and Boundaries*. Oslo, Universitetsforlaget.

BLACK, W. R.
1960 "The Labrador Floater Fishery." *Annals of the Association of American Geographers*, 50(3):267–293.

BRIGGS, JEAN L.
1970 *Never in Anger: Portrait of an Eskimo Family*. Cambridge, Mass., Harvard University Press.

BROX, OTTAR
1972 *Newfoundland Fishermen in the Age of Industry. A Sociology of Economic Dualism*. St. John's, Institute of Social and Economic Research, Memorial University of Newfoundland.

CAVAN, RUTH SHONLE and KATHERINE H. RANCK
1938 *The Family and the Depression*. Chicago, University of Chicago Press.

CAVAN, RUTH SHONLE (ed.)
1959 *Marriage & Family in the Modern World*. Third Edition, New York, Thomas Y. Crowell Co.

CHIARAMONTE, LOUIS J.
1971 *Craftsman-Client Contracts: Interpersonal Relations in a Newfoundland Fishing Community*. St. John's, Institute of Social and Economic Research, Memorial University of Newfoundland.

CLOWARD, RICHARD A. and FRANCIS FOX PIVEN
1965 "Politics, the Welfare System, and Poverty." In L. A. Ferman, J. L. Kornbluh, and A. Haber (eds.), *Poverty in America*. Ann Arbor, University of Michigan Press.

COPES, P.
1964 "Government Assistance, Productivity and Income in the Fishing Industry of Newfoundland." Memorial University of Newfoundland. Mimeograph.

CURRAN, JOHN P.
1971 "The Process of Mechanization of the Forest Industry of New-foundland." Unpublished M.A. Thesis. Memorial University of Newfoundland.

DEMAS, W. G.
1965 *The Economics of Development in Small Countries, with Special Reference to the Caribbean.* Montreal, McGill University Press.

DYKE, A. P.
1968 "Subsistence Production in the Household Economy of Rural New-foundland." In Michael L. Skolnik (ed.), *Viewpoints on Communities in Crisis.* St. John's, Institute of Social and Economic Research, Memorial University of Newfoundland.

ECONOMIC COUNCIL OF CANADA
1968 *Fifth Annual Review: The Challenge of Growth and Change.* Ottawa, Queen's Printer.

EDGECOMBE, ROBERTA
1967 "The Newfoundland Inshore Cod Fishery: A Study of Resource Allocation." Unpublished M.A. Thesis. University of British Columbia.

EIDHEIM, HARALD
1971 *Aspects of the Lappish Minority Situation.* Oslo, Universitetsforlaget.

EVENING TELEGRAM
St. John's daily newspaper.

FARIS, JAMES C.
1966 *Cat Harbour: A Newfoundland Fishing Settlement.* St. John's, Institute of Social and Economic Research, Memorial University of Newfoundland. (2nd ed., 1972)

FELTHAM, JOHN
1959 "The Development of the Fisherman's Protective Union in New-foundland (1908–1923)." Unpublished M.A. Thesis. Memorial University of Newfoundland.

FIRESTONE, MELVIN M.
1967 *Brothers and Rivals: Patrilocality in Savage Cove.* St. John's, Institute of Social and Economic Research, Memorial University of Newfoundland.

GLADWIN, THOMAS
1967 *Poverty U.S.A.* Boston/Toronto, Little, Brown & Co.

GOFFMAN, ERVING
1959 *The Presentation of Self in Everyday Life.* Garden City, New York, Doubleday and Co.

GOFFMAN, ERVING
1961 *Encounters: Two Studies in the Sociology of Interaction.* Indianapolis, Bobbs-Merrill Co.

GOFFMAN, ERVING
  1963 *Stigma: Notes on the Management of Spoiled Identity*. Englewood
  Cliffs, N.J., Prentice Hall, Inc.
GOLDSTEIN, BERNARD
  1967 *Low Income Youth in Urban Areas: a Critical Review of the Litera-
  ture*. New York, Holt, Rinehart and Winston, Inc.
GOULDNER, ALWIN W.
  1954 *Patterns of Industrial Bureaucracy*. Glencoe, Ill., Free Press.
HANNERZ, ULF
  1969 *Soulside: Inquiries into Ghetto Culture and Community*. New York
  and London, Columbia University Press.
HIRSCHMAN, A. O.
  1958 *The Strategy of Economic Development*. New Haven, Yale Uni-
  versity Press.
HURWITZ, NATHAN
  1966 "Seasonal Unemployment in the Province." *The Newfoundland
  Journal of Commerce,* September, 1966.
IVERSON, NOEL and D. RALPH MATTHEWS
  1967 *Communities in Decline: An Examination of Household Resettle-
  ment in Newfoundland*. St. John's, Institute of Social and Economic
  Research, Memorial University of Newfoundland.
KITCHEN, H. W.
  1969 "Education Policy for the Seventies for Newfoundland." Memorial
  University of Newfoundland. Mimeograph.
LIEBOW, ELLIOT
  1967 *Tally's Corner: a Study of Negro Streetcorner Men*. Boston/To-
  ronto, Little, Brown and Co.
MAUSS, MARCEL
  1967 *The Gift. Forms and Functions of Exchange in Archaic Societies*.
  New York, W. W. Norton and Co.
MCKAY, R. A. (ed.)
  1946 *Newfoundland: Economic, Diplomatic, and Strategic Studies*. To-
  ronto, Oxford University Press.
MOWAT, FARLEY and JOHN DE VISSER
  1968 *This Rock Within the Sea: A Heritage Lost*. Boston/Toronto, Little,
  Brown and Co.
NADEL, SIEGFRIED F.
  1957 *The Theory of Social Structure*. London, Cohen & West.
NEWFOUNDLAND
  1933 *Report of the Newfoundland Royal Commission* (The Amulree
  Report). London, His Majesty's Stationery Office.
NEWFOUNDLAND
  1950–1969 *Department of Public Welfare. Annual Reports*. St. John's,
  Government of Newfoundland and Labrador.

NEWFOUNDLAND

1967 *Report of the Royal Commission on the Economic State and Prospects of Newfoundland and Labrador.* St. John's, Queen's Printer.

NEWFOUNDLAND

1967–68 *Report of the Royal Commission on Education and Youth.* Vol. I and II, St. John's, Queen's Printer.

NEWFOUNDLAND

1968 "Government of Newfoundland and Labrador: Budget Speech." Department of Finance. Mimeograph.

PAINE, ROBERT

1969 "In Search of Friendship: an Exploratory Analysis in 'Middleclass' Culture." *Man,* 4(4):505–524.

PERLIN, A. B.

1959 *The Story of Newfoundland.* St. John's, The Guardian Limited.

PETERS, R. D.

1967 "The Social and Economic Effects of the Transition from a System of Woodcamps to a System of Commuting in the Newfoundland Pulpwood Industry." Unpublished M.A. Thesis. Memorial University of Newfoundland.

PHILBROOK, T.

1966 *Fisherman, Logger, Merchant, Miner: Social Change and Industrialism in Three Newfoundland Communities.* St. John's, Institute of Social and Economic Research, Memorial University of Newfoundland.

PITT-RIVERS, JULIAN

1961 "Interpersonal Relations in a Peasant Society: a Comment." *Human Organization,* 19:180–183.

ROBB, A. L. and R. EDGECOMBE ROBB

1969 "A Cost-Benefit Analysis of the Newfoundland Resettlement Program." Institute of Social and Economic Research, Memorial University of Newfoundland. Mimeograph.

ROWE, F. W.

1964 *The Development of Education in Newfoundland.* Toronto, Ryerson Press.

ROWE, F. W.

1967 "People Who Want to Move." *The Atlantic Advocate,* October, 1967.

SAHLINS, M. D.

1965 "On the Sociology of Primitive Exchange." In M. Banton (ed.), *The Relevance of Models for Social Anthropology.* ASA monographs, no. 1, London, Tavistock.

SINGH, B.

1964 "Demand for Agricultural Products." Agricultural Rural Development Act Project No. 7. Newfoundland Department of Mines, Agriculture, and Resources. Mimeograph.

SKOLNIK, MICHAEL, L.

1966 "Some Aspects of the Theory and Measurement of Economics of Scale." Unpublished B.Phil. Thesis. University of Oxford.

SKOLNIK, MICHAEL L. (ed.)

1968 *Viewpoints on Communities in Crisis.* St. John's, Institute of Social and Economic Research, Memorial University of Newfoundland.

SKOLNIK, MICHAEL L. and CATO WADEL

1969 "Occupational Pluralism as an Adaptation to Rural Unemployment: The Case of Newfoundland." Institute of Social and Economic Research, Memorial University of Newfoundland. Mimeograph.

STAVELEY, MICHAEL

n.d. "Newfoundland Census Material." Institute of Social and Economic Research, Memorial University of Newfoundland. Mimeograph.

STEBBINS, ROBERT A.

1970 "On Misunderstanding the Concept of Commitment: A Theoretical Clarification." *Social Forces,* 48(4).

SZWED, JOHN

1966 *Private Cultures and Public Imagery: Interpersonal Relations in a Newfoundland Peasant Society.* St. John's, Institute of Social and Economic Research, Memorial University of Newfoundland.

WADEL, CATO

1969a *Marginal Adaptations and Modernization in Newfoundland: a Study of Strategies and Implications of Resettlement and Redevelopment of Outport Fishing Communities.* St. John's, Institute of Social and Economic Research, Memorial University of Newfoundland.

WADEL, CATO

1969b "Communities and Committees. Community Development and the Enlargement of the Sense of Community on Fogo Island, Newfoundland." Extension Service, Memorial University of Newfoundland. Mimeograph.

WISE, T. F.

n.d. "Budgets, Credit and Skills. Survey of Rural Fishermen." Agricultural Rural Development Act Project No. 1022. St. John's. Mimeograph.

WOLF, ERIC R.

1955 "Types of Latin American Peasantry: A Preliminary Discussion." *American Anthropologist,* 57:452–471.

WOLF, ERIC R.

1966 *Peasants.* Englewood Cliffs, N.J., Prentice Hall.

ISER Publications

Studies

1 TOM PHILBROOK. *Fisherman, Logger, Merchant, Miner: Social Change and Industrialism in Three Newfoundland Communities*

2 JOHN SZWED. *Private Cultures and Public Imagery: Interpersonal Relations in a Newfoundland Peasant Society*

3 JAMES C. FARIS. *Cat Harbour: A Newfoundland Fishing Settlement*

4 SHMUEL BEN-DOR. *Makkovik: Eskimos and Settlers in a Labrador Community*

5 MELVIN M. FIRESTONE. *Brothers and Rivals: Patrilocality in Savage Cove*

6 NOEL IVERSON and D. RALPH MATTHEWS. *Communities in Decline: An Examination of Household Resettlement in Newfoundland*

7 CATO WADEL. *Marginal Adaptations and Modernization in Newfoundland: A Study of Strategies and Implications of Resettlement and Redevelopment of Outport Fishing Communities*

8 ROBERT L. DEWITT. *Public Policy and Community Protest: The Fogo Case*

9 OTTAR BROX. *Newfoundland Fishermen in the Age of Industry: A Sociology of Economic Dualism*

10 LOUIS J. CHIARAMONTE. *Craftsman-client Contracts: Interpersonal Relations in a Newfoundland Fishing Community*

11 CATO WADEL. *Now Whose Fault is That? The Struggle for Self-Esteem in the Face of Chronic Unemployment*

12 GEORG HENRIKSEN. *Hunters in the Barrens: The Naskapi on the Edge of the White Man's World*

13 ROBERT MCGHEE. *Beluga Hunters: An Archaeological Reconstruction of the history and culture of the Mackenzie Delta Kittegaryumiut*

14 A.P. COHEN. *The Management of Myths. The Politics of Legitimation in a Newfoundland Community*

15 ELLIOTT LEYTON. *The One Blood: Kinship and Class in an Irish Village*

16 DAVID W. ZIMMERLY. *Cain's Land Revisited: Culture Change in Central Labrador, 1775-1972*

17 JAMES A. TUCK. *Ancient People of Port au Choix: The Excavation of an Archaic Indian Cemetery in Newfoundland*

18 S.S. MENSINKAI and M.Q. DALVI. *Manpower and Educational Development in Newfoundland*

19 DAVID ALEXANDER. *The Decay of Trade: An Economic History of the Newfoundland Saltfish Trade, 1935-1965*

20 PAUL S. DINHAM. *You Never Know What They Might Do: Mental Illness in Outport Newfoundland*

Papers

Other